Book E

LANGUAGE
Power

gagelearning

Copyright © 2002 Gage Learning Corporation

1120 Birchmount Road, Toronto, Ontario M1K 5G4 1-800-668-0671

www.nelson.com

Adapted from material developed, designed, and copyrighted by Steck-Vaughn

We acknowledge the financial support of the Government of Canada through the Book Publishing Industry Development Program for our publishing activities.

We acknowledge the Government of Ontario through the Ontario Media Development Corporation's Ontario Book Initiative.

Editorial Team: Chelsea Donaldson, Carol Waldock

Cover Adaptation: Christine Dandurand

ISBN **0-7715-1017-9**

2 3 4 5 MP 06 05 04 03

Printed and bound in Canada

Table of Contents

Unit 6 Study Skills

Final Reviews

Lesson 1

Synonyms and Antonyms

> ▪ A **synonym** is a word that has the same or nearly the same meaning as one or more other words.   EXAMPLES: reply – answer   talk – speak

A. Write a synonym for each word below.

1. pleasant _____

2. enough _____

3. leave _____

4. inquire _____

5. fearless _____

6. artificial _____

7. famous _____

8. trade _____

9. house _____

10. nation _____

11. difficult _____

12. vacant _____

B. Write four sentences about recycling. In each sentence, use a synonym for the word in parentheses. Underline the synonym.

1. (packaging) _____

2. (waste) _____

3. (landfill) _____

4. (planet) _____

> ▪ An **antonym** is a word that has the opposite meaning of another word.
> EXAMPLES: old—new   bad—good

C. Write an antonym for each word below.

1. failure _____

2. absent _____

3. before _____

4. slow _____

5. all _____

6. forget _____

7. love _____

8. no _____

9. friend _____

10. always _____

11. light _____

12. forward _____

D. In each sentence, write an antonym for the word in parentheses that makes sense in the sentence.

1. Thao ran his hand along the (smooth) _____ surface of the wood.

2. He knew he would have to (stop) _____ sanding it.

3. Only after sanding would he be able to (destroy) _____ a table.

4. He would try to (forget) _____ not to sand it too much.

Lesson 2

Homonyms

> - A **homonym** is a word that sounds the same as another word but has a different spelling and a different meaning.
>   EXAMPLES: aisle – I'll – isle   flower – flour

A. Underline the correct homonym(s) in each sentence below.

1. The (two, too, to) people walked very slowly (passed, past) the house.

2. The children were (two, too, to) tired (two, too, to) talk.

3. Did you (hear, here) that noise?

4. Yes, I (heard, herd) it.

5. I do (knot, not) (know, no) of a person who is (knot, not) ready to help the hungry people of the world.

6. Michelle, you (seam, seem) to have forgotten about (our, hour) plans for the picnic.

7. Who (won, one) the citizenship (medal, meddle) this year?

8. Jim, how much do you (way, weigh)?

9. The night (air, heir) is (sew, so) cool that you will (knead, need) a light jacket.

10. The small plants were set out in orderly (rows, rose).

11. I (knew, new) those (knew, new) shoes would hurt my (feat, feet).

12. Which countries lead in the production of (beat, beet) sugar?

13. We did (not, knot) go to the (seen, scene) of the wreck.

14. Sue wore the belt around her (waist, waste).

B. Write a homonym for each word below.

1. peace _____
2. altar _____
3. to _____
4. way _____
5. beech _____
6. plain _____
7. coarse _____
8. seem _____
9. knew _____
10. sale _____

11. sew _____
12. break _____
13. week _____
14. rein _____
15. bare _____
16. scene _____
17. mite _____
18. whole _____
19. hoarse _____
20. fourth _____

21. knight _____
22. hymn _____
23. through _____
24. grown _____
25. wrap _____
26. prey _____
27. strait _____
28. sole _____
29. hear _____
30. ware _____

Homographs

> ▪ A **homograph** is a word that has the same spelling as another word but a different meaning and sometimes a different pronunciation.
> EXAMPLE: <u>saw</u>, meaning "have seen," and <u>saw</u>, meaning "a tool used for cutting"

A. Circle the letter for the definition that best defines each underlined homograph.

1. Sara jumped at the <u>bangs</u> of the exploding balloons.
   a. fringe of hair **b.** loud noises

2. She grabbed a stick to <u>arm</u> herself against the threat.
   a. part of the body **b.** take up a weapon

3. The dog's <u>bark</u> woke the family.
   a. noise a dog makes **b.** outside covering on a tree

4. Mix the pancake <u>batter</u> for three minutes.
   a. person at bat **b.** mixture for cooking

B. Use the homographs in the box to complete the sentences below. Each homograph will be used twice.

1. Pieces of a board game are _____ .

   People who are cashiers are _____ .

2. A water bird is a _____ .

   To lower the head is to _____ .

3. A metal container is a _____ .

   If you are able, you _____ .

4. To get down from something is to _____ .

   If something is on fire, it is _____ .

> duck
>
> alight
>
> can
>
> checkers

C. Write the homograph for each pair of meanings below. The first letter of each word is given for you.

1. **a.** building for horses **b.** delay s _____

2. **a.** a metal fastener **b.** a sound made with fingers s _____

3. **a.** to crush **b.** a yellow vegetable s _____

4. **a.** to otop eating **b.** quickly f _____

5. **a.** to strike **b.** a party fruit drink p _____

- A **prefix** added to the beginning of a base word changes the meaning of the word.

  EXAMPLE: <u>dis-</u>, meaning "opposite of," + the base word <u>appear</u> = disappear, meaning "the opposite of appear"

  EXAMPLES:

prefix	meaning	prefix	meaning
in-	not	re-	again
dis-	not	fore-	before
un-	not	pre-	before
trans-	across	mis-	wrong
		with-	from, against

- **Write a new word using one of the prefixes listed above. Then write the meaning of the new word.**

WORD	NEW WORD	MEANING
1. fair		
2. justice		
3. tell		
4. warn		
5. visible		
6. spell		
7. agree		
8. see		
9. behave		
10. stand		
11. complete		
12. please		
13. drawn		
14. likely		
15. match		
16. clean		
17. understand		
18. correct		

- A **suffix** added to the end of a base word changes the meaning of the word.

  EXAMPLE: -less, meaning "without," + the base word worth = worthless, meaning "without worth"

  EXAMPLES:

suffix	meaning	suffix	meaning
-less	without	-ist	one skilled in
-ish	of the nature of	-tion	art of
-ous	full of	-ful	full of
-en	to make	-al	pertaining to
-hood	state of being	-able	able to be
-ward	in the direction of	-ible	able to be
-ness	quality of		

- Sometimes you need to change the spelling of a base word when a suffix is added.

  EXAMPLE: happy – happiness

- Write a new word using one of the suffixes listed above. Then write the meaning of the new word.

WORD	NEW WORD	MEANING
1. care	_____	_____
2. truth	_____	_____
3. fame	_____	_____
4. soft	_____	_____
5. down	_____	_____
6. light	_____	_____
7. east	_____	_____
8. honour	_____	_____
9. thank	_____	_____
10. rest	_____	_____
11. child	_____	_____
12. remark	_____	_____
13. violin	_____	_____
14. courage	_____	_____
15. worth	_____	_____

Contractions

- A **contraction** is a word formed by joining two other words.
- An **apostrophe** shows where a letter or letters have been omitted.
    EXAMPLE: had not = hadn't
- <u>Won't</u> is an exception.
    EXAMPLE: Will not = won't

A. Write the contraction for each pair of words.

1. did not _____
2. was not _____
3. we are _____
4. is not _____
5. who is _____
6. had not _____
7. I will _____
8. I am _____
9. it is _____
10. do not _____

11. they have _____
12. would not _____
13. will not _____
14. does not _____
15. were not _____
16. there is _____
17. could not _____
18. I have _____
19. she will _____
20. they are _____

B. Underline each contraction. Write the words that make up the contraction on the lines.

1. They're dusting the piano very carefully before they inspect it. _____

2. They'll want to look closely, in case there are any scratches. _____

3. If it's in good condition, Mary will buy it. _____

4. Mary's an excellent piano player. _____

5. Her friends think she'll earn a university scholarship with her talent. _____

6. Tom doesn't play the piano, but he's a great cook. _____ _____

7. He'd like to be a professional chef. _____

8. His friends would've liked for him to go to university. _____

9. But they aren't concerned as long as Tom's happy. _____ _____

10. Tom and Mary think they've got very supportive friends. _____

Lesson 7 — Compound Words

- A **compound word** is a word that is made up of two or more words. The meaning of many compound words is related to the meaning of each individual word.

  EXAMPLE: blue + berry = blueberry, meaning "a type of berry that is blue"

- Compound words may be written as one word, as hyphenated words, or as two separate words. Always check a dictionary.

A. Combine the words in the list to make compound words. You may use words more than once.

| air | knob | door | port | paper | condition | black | berry |
| sand | line | stand | under | way | ground | bird | sea |

1. _____
2. _____
3. _____
4. _____
5. _____
6. _____
7. _____
8. _____
9. _____
10. _____
11. _____
12. _____

B. Answer the following questions.

1. Whirl means "to move in circles." What is a whirlpool?

   _____

2. Since quick means "moves rapidly," what is quicksand?

   _____

3. Rattle means "to make sharp, short sounds quickly." What is a rattlesnake?

   _____

4. A ring is "a small, circular band." What is an earring?

   _____

5. Pool can mean "a group of people who do something together." What is a car pool?

   _____

6. A lace can be "a string or cord that is used to hold something together." What is a shoelace?

   _____

Connotation/Denotation

> - The **denotation** of a word is its exact meaning as stated in a dictionary.
>   - EXAMPLE: The denotation of stingy is "ungenerous" or "miserly."
> - The **connotation** of a word is an added meaning that suggests something positive or negative.
>   - EXAMPLES: **Negative:** Stingy suggests "ungenerous." Stingy has a negative connotation.
>
>   **Positive:** Economical suggests "efficient" and "careful." Economical has a positive connotation.
> - Some words are neutral. They do not suggest either good or bad feelings.
>   - EXAMPLES: garage, kitchen, roof

A. Write (−) if the underlined word has a negative connotation. Write (+) if it has a positive connotation. Write (N) if the word is neutral.

_____ 1. This is my house.

_____ 2. This is my home.

_____ 3. Darren's friends discussed his problem.

_____ 4. Darren's friends gossiped about his problem.

_____ 5. Our dog is sick.

_____ 6. Our dog is diseased.

_____ 7. The play was enjoyable.

_____ 8. The play was fantastic.

_____ 9. Julie is boring.

_____ 10. Julie is quiet.

B. Fill each blank with the word that suggests the connotation given.

1. Our experience of the storm was _____ . (negative)

2. Our experience of the storm was _____ . (positive)

3. Our experience of the storm was _____ . (neutral)

unpleasant
exciting
horrible

4. Monica is _____ . (neutral)

5. Monica is _____ . (positive)

6. Monica is _____ . (negative)

old
over-the-hill
mature

- An **idiom** is an expression that has a meaning different from the usual meanings of the individual words within it.
    EXAMPLE: Lit a fire under me means "got me going," not "burned me."

A. Underline the idiom in each sentence. Then write what the idiom means.

1. Jack and Ellen knew they were in hot water when their car died.

   _____

2. They were a long way from any town, and Ellen was beside herself.

   _____

3. Jack said they should put their heads together and find a solution.

   _____

4. Ellen told Jack that if he had any ideas, she was all ears.

   _____

5. Jack told her it was too soon to throw in the towel.

   _____

B. Underline each idiom. Then write one definition that tells the exact meaning of the phrase and another definition that tells what the phrase means in the sentence.

1. When I finish the test, I'm going to hit the road.

   a. ___Pound on the street_____

   b. ___Leave_____

2. I had to eat crow when I found out I was wrong about the test date.

   a. _____

   b. _____

3. With final exams coming, I'll have to burn the midnight oil.

   a. _____

   b. _____

4. I thought I was so smart, but that test really cut me down to size.

   a. _____

   b. _____

A. Write S before each pair of synonyms. Write A before each pair of antonyms.

_____ 1. quiet, noisy   _____ 5. healthy, sick   _____ 9. fast, quick

_____ 2. fearless, brave   _____ 6. calm, peaceful   _____ 10. cry, weep

_____ 3. begin, start   _____ 7. lost, found   _____ 11. bottom, top

_____ 4. gentle, rough   _____ 8. night, day   _____ 12. dull, sharp

B. Using the homonyms in parentheses, write the correct words on the lines.

1. (week, weak)   Anna was _____ for a _____ after she had the flu.

2. (right, write)   Did you _____ down the _____ address?

3. (blew, blue)   The wind _____ leaves and twigs into the beautiful _____ water.

4. (read, red)   Meg _____ a poem about a young girl with _____ hair and freckles.

5. (pane, pain)   Maria felt a _____ in her hand when she tried to remove the broken

   window _____ .

C. Circle the letter of the best definition for each underlined homograph.

1. John <u>flies</u> to Calgary every summer to visit his family.

   a. insects   **b.** moves in the air

2. Mr. Bailey owns a fruit and vegetable <u>stand</u>.

   a . to be on one's feet   **b.** a small, open structure

3. The band enjoyed performing at the <u>ball</u>.

   a. a large formal dance   **b.** a round body or object

4. Don't forget to <u>wind</u> the alarm clock before you go to bed.

   a. air movement   **b.** to tighten a spring

D. Choose an appropriate prefix or suffix from the box for each of the underlined words below. Write the new word on the line.

| dis-   mis-   re-   un-   -ish   -ful   -less   -en |

1. full of <u>thanks</u> _____   5. to make <u>black</u> _____

2. to <u>pay</u> again _____   6. without <u>thanks</u> _____

3. to not <u>agree</u> _____   7. not <u>happy</u> _____

4. act as a <u>fool</u> _____   8. <u>take</u> wrongly _____

E. Underline the pair of words that can be written as a contraction in each sentence. Then write each contraction on the line.

_____ 1. Yolanda does not want to work late today.

_____ 2. She would rather come in early tomorrow.

_____ 3. It is getting dark.

_____ 4. She does not like driving in the dark.

_____ 5. You must not blame her.

_____ 6. Who is going to stay with her?

_____ 7. James did not volunteer.

F. Combine two words in each sentence to make a compound word. Write the word on the line.

1. I polished the brass knob on the door. _____

2. Lynn rested her swollen foot on the stool. _____

3. The police tried to block the road to catch the thief. _____

4. Please walk on the left side of the street. _____

5. I keep my green plants in my warm house during the winter. _____

G. Write (−) if the underlined word has a negative connotation. Write (+) if the underlined word has a positive connotation.

_____ 1. Stavros is sometimes <u>narrow-minded</u>.   _____ 6. The child <u>grabbed</u> the toy and ran away.

_____ 2. Marie is very <u>outgoing</u>.   _____ 7. Those insects are real <u>pests</u>.

_____ 3. Do you like to <u>gossip</u>?   _____ 8. I <u>demand</u> that you listen to me.

_____ 4. Carla can <u>gab</u> for hours.   _____ 9. The <u>mansion</u> was very old.

_____ 5. Let's <u>donate</u> this later.   _____ 10. Steve drives an old <u>jalopy</u>.

H. Underline the idiom in each sentence. Then write what the idiom means.

1. Since there was little time, the mayor only hit the high spots of his speech.

_____

2. The committee's bank account was low, so they had to cut corners on their party.

_____

3. Mark couldn't find a job, so he asked his uncle to pull some strings for him.

_____

Using What You've Learned

A. On the line before each sentence, write <u>synonym</u>, <u>antonym</u>, <u>homonym</u>, or <u>homograph</u> to describe the pair of underlined words.

_____ **1.** You may give an <u>answer</u>, but be sure of your <u>reply</u>.

_____ **2.** <u>Be</u> very careful in your explanation of the <u>bee</u>.

_____ **3.** The <u>bank</u> on the river <u>bank</u> refused my request for a loan.

_____ **4.** I <u>ate</u> dinner at <u>eight</u> last night.

_____ **5.** <u>Look</u> in the closet to <u>see</u> if my protective suit is there.

_____ **6.** Randy knew the <u>answer</u> to the <u>question</u> about bee colonies.

_____ **7.** Why are you making such a <u>big</u> fuss over such a <u>little</u> thing?

B. In each sentence, underline the word that contains a prefix or a suffix. Then write a definition of that word.

1. Jiro was thankful for a chance to play.

_____

2. Connie was very unhappy about missing the ball.

_____

3. The coach was displeased at our performance.

_____

4. It was a thankless job, but someone had to clean up the park.

_____

5. We repainted the bleachers this summer.

_____

6. We will transplant flower bulbs this fall.

_____

7. We were unsure that it would be done by Saturday.

_____

C. Write the words that make up each contraction below.

1. won't _____   **3.** it's _____   **5.** she'll _____

2. I'm _____   **4.** weren't _____   **6.** we're _____

D. Write (–) if the definition has a negative connotation. Write (N) if the definition is neutral.

1. **desert** _____ leave _____ abandon

2. **curious** _____ nosy; prying _____ eager to know

3. **clown** _____ circus performer _____ silly actor

4. **jungle** _____ hectic, crowded place _____ place with much plant growth

5. **anxious** _____ concerned _____ nervous; full of fear

6. **fall** _____ drop _____ plunge

7. **look** _____ view _____ stare; gawk

8. **response** _____ excuse _____ explanation

E. Rewrite the paragraph. Replace the idioms with other words or phrases that have the same meaning as the idioms.

"I'd take the rumour about the test with a grain of salt," Tom said. "Our teacher knows we're on top of the world about the class party. I'm sure she wouldn't knock the pins out from under us by making us hit the books now for a test. We've been trying to find out, but she hasn't spilled the beans yet. Maybe we'd better stop beating around the bush and ask her. I'd hate to end up just taking a shot in the dark on an important test."

_____

_____

_____

_____

_____

_____

_____

_____

_____

_____

_____

_____

Recognizing Sentences

> ■ A **sentence** is a group of words that expresses a complete thought.
> EXAMPLE: We found a deserted cabin at the top of the hill.

■ **Some of the following groups of words are sentences, and some are not. Write S before each group that is a sentence. Punctuate each sentence with a period.**

_____ 1. Tomás did not go to the auto show ____

_____ 2. By the side of the babbling brook ____

_____ 3. I went to the new museum last week ____

_____ 4. Mile after mile along the great highway ____

_____ 5. Check all work carefully ____

_____ 6. Down the narrow aisle of the church ____

_____ 7. I have lost my hat ____

_____ 8. On our way to work this morning ____

_____ 9. Leonard Cohen, a famous singer ____

_____ 10. We saw Katherine and Sheryl yesterday ____

_____ 11. The severe cold of last winter ____

_____ 12. Once upon a time, long, long ago ____

_____ 13. There was a gorgeous sunset last night ____

_____ 14. He ran home ____

_____ 15. My brother and my sister ____

_____ 16. Tom and Matt did a great job ____

_____ 17. We saw a beaver in the deep ravine ____

_____ 18. The cat in our neighbour's yard ____

_____ 19. Every year at the science fair ____

_____ 20. As we came to the sharp curve in the road ____

_____ 21. Just before we were ready ____

_____ 22. I heard that you and Lorenzo have a new paper route ____

_____ 23. Longfellow is called the children's poet ____

_____ 24. Into the parking garage ____

_____ 25. We washed and waxed the truck ____

_____ 26. Through the door and up the stairs ____

_____ 27. As quickly as possible ____

_____ 28. We saw the new killer whale at the zoo ____

_____ 29. Patel parked the car on the street ____

_____ 30. We had ice cream and fruit for dessert ____

Types of Sentences

- A **declarative sentence** makes a statement. It is followed by a period (.).
    EXAMPLE: Alicia is my cousin.
- An **interrogative sentence** asks a question. It is followed by a question mark (?).   EXAMPLE: Where are you going?
- An **imperative sentence** expresses a command or request. It is followed by a period (.).   EXAMPLE: Close the door.
- An **exclamatory sentence** expresses strong emotion. It can also express a command or request that is made with great excitement. It is followed by an exclamation mark (!).   EXAMPLES: How you frightened me! Look at that accident!

A. Write D for declarative, IN for interrogative, IM for imperative, or E for exclamatory before each sentence. Put the correct punctuation at the end of each sentence.

_____ 1. Everyone will be here by nine o'clock ___

_____ 2. Train your mind to do its work efficiently ___

_____ 3. How does a canal lock work ___

_____ 4. Prepare each day's assignment on time ___

_____ 5. Are we going to the game now ___

_____ 6. Who brought these delicious peaches ___

_____ 7. Our guests have arrived ___

_____ 8. What is meant by rotation of crops ___

_____ 9. Please bring a glass of water ___

_____ 10. Stop that noise ___

_____ 11. Always stand erect ___

_____ 12. Who arranged these flowers ___

_____ 13. Savitsa, what do you have in that box ___

_____ 14. The Vikings were famous sailors ___

_____ 15. Have you solved all the problems in our lesson ___

_____ 16. Roland, hand me that wrench ___

_____ 17. What is the capital of Nova Scotia ___

_____ 18. Cultivate a pleasant manner ___

_____ 19. How is a pizza made ___

_____ 20. Block that kick ___

_____ 21. A nation is measured by the character of its people ___

_____ 22. Are you an early riser ___

_____ 23. Practise good table manners ___

_____ 24. What a wonderful time we've had ___

_____ 25. How did you get here so early ___

_____ 26. Look out for those cars ___

_____ 27. Take good care of my dog ___

_____ 28. There are many grain silos in our province ___

_____ 29. Name the capital of Newfoundland ___

_____ 30. Hurrah, the game is over ___

_____ 31. Draw a map of South America ___

_____ 32. Geysers were first discovered in Iceland ___

_____ 33. Have you ever been on a roller coaster ___

_____ 34. Sweep the front walk ___

_____ 35. Do not measure people by what they have ___

_____ 36. Many hands make light work ___

_____ 37. Jon Vickers has sung with many of the major opera companies ___

_____ 38. What is the longest river in the country ___

_____ 39. Oh, you have a new car ___

_____ 40. Andrea, why weren't you at the meeting ___

_____ 41. The organization will elect officers tomorrow ___

_____ 42. Chris, I have a long piece of twine ___

_____ 43. Paul, jump quickly ___

B. Only one group of words in each pair below is a sentence. Circle the sentence, and tell what kind it is. Write D for declarative, IN for interrogative, IM for imperative, or E for exclamatory.

_____ 1. When will the train arrive? Two hours late.

_____ 2. It is delayed by bad weather. Not here yet.

_____ 3. From Alberta. Josiah and Shelly are on it.

_____ 4. I haven't seen them in two years! Am waiting patiently.

_____ 5. Enjoy travelling. They will stay with us for two weeks.

_____ 6. We have many things planned for them. A good visit.

_____ 7. Sleep in the guest room. To our city's new zoo?

_____ 8. Josiah used to work at a zoo. Many animals.

_____ 9. Go in the reptile house. Took care of the elephants.

_____ 10. Each elephant had a name. Wally, Sandra, and Joe.

_____ 11. The elephants liked to train with Josiah. Good job.

_____ 12. Sandra, the elephant, had a baby. In the zoo.

_____ 13. Male elephant. What did the zoo officials name the baby?

_____ 14. People in the zoo. They surprised Josiah!

_____ 15. He never had an elephant named for him before! Seal exhibit.

 Unit 2, Sentences

- Every sentence has two main parts, a **complete subject** and a **complete predicate**.
- The complete subject includes all the words that tell who or what the sentence is about. EXAMPLE: **All chickadees**/hunt insect eggs.
- The complete predicate includes all the words that state the action or condition of the subject. EXAMPLE: All chickadees/**hunt insect eggs**.

A. Draw a line between the complete subject and the complete predicate in each sentence below.

1. Amy/built a bird feeder for the backyard.
2. This cleaner will remove paint.
3. Many beautiful waltzes were composed by Johann Strauss.
4. Queen Victoria ruled England for many years.
5. Eighty people are waiting in line for tickets.
6. Mario's last visit was during the summer.
7. The rocket was soon in orbit.
8. Our last meeting was held in my living room.
9. The farmers are harvesting their wheat.
10. Our new house has six rooms.
11. The heart pumps blood throughout the body.
12. This computer will help you work faster.
13. My friend has moved to Saint Foy, Québec.
14. A deep silence fell upon the crowd.
15. The police officers were stopping the speeding motorists.
16. The French chef prepared excellent food.
17. My father is a mechanic.
18. Pierre Leblanc is running for the city council.
19. Lightning struck a tree in our yard.
20. Magazines about bicycling are becoming increasingly popular.
21. They answered every question honestly during the interview.
22. The grey twilight came before the program ended.
23. Steve has a way with words.
24. That section of the country has many pine forests.
25. We will have a party for Teresa on Friday.
26. Butterflies flew around the flowers.
27. The heavy bus was stuck in the mud.

B. Write a sentence by adding a complete predicate to each complete subject.

1. All of the students _____

2. Elephants _____

3. The top of the mountain _____

4. The television programs tonight _____

5. I _____

6. Each of the girls _____

7. My father's truck _____

8. The dam across the river _____

9. Our new station wagon _____

10. You _____

11. The books in our bookcase _____

12. The mountains _____

13. Today's paper _____

14. The magazine staff _____

C. Write a sentence by adding a complete subject to each complete predicate.

1. _____ is the largest city in Mexico.

2. _____ came to our program.

3. _____ is a valuable mineral.

4. _____ grow beside the road.

5. _____ travelled day and night.

6. _____ was a great inventor.

7. _____ wrote the letter of complaint.

8. _____ met us at the airport.

9. _____ made ice cream for the picnic.

10. _____ made a nest in our tree.

11. _____ lives near the shopping centre.

12. _____ have a meeting on Saturday.

    Unit 2, Sentences

> ■ The **simple subject** of a sentence is the main word in the complete subject. The simple subject is a noun or a pronoun. Sometimes the simple subject is also the complete subject.   EXAMPLES: Our **car**/swayed in the strong wind. **Cars**/sway in the strong wind.

A. Draw a line between the complete subject and the complete predicate in each sentence below. Then underline the simple subject.

1. The plants sprouted quickly after the first rain.
2. The television program was very informative.
3. I used a word processor to write the paper.
4. My friend's truck is parked in the driveway.
5. The beavers created a dam in the river.
6. The books lined the shelves like toy soldiers.
7. Hail pounded against the storm door.
8. I bought a new mountain bike.
9. My favourite subject is history.
10. The colourful bird sang a beautiful melody.
11. The tree trunk was about two metres in diameter.
12. The sidewalk had cracks in the pavement.

> ■ The **simple predicate** of a sentence is a verb within the complete predicate. The simple predicate may be made up of one word or more than one word.
> EXAMPLES: Our car/**swayed**. The wind/**was blowing** hard.

B. In each sentence below, draw a line between the complete subject and the complete predicate. Underline the simple predicate twice.

1. A rare Chinese vase was on display.
2. Many of the children had played.
3. All of the group went on a hike.
4. He drove the bus slowly over the slippery pavement.
5. A large number of water-skiers were on the lake last Saturday.
6. Birds have good eyesight.
7. Who discovered the Pacific Ocean?
8. I am reading the assignment now.
9. The glare of the headlights blinded us.
10. The problem on the next page is harder.

- When the subject of a sentence comes before the verb, the sentence is in **natural order**.   EXAMPLE: Maria went home.
- When the verb or part of the verb comes before the subject, the sentence is in **inverted order**.   EXAMPLES: On the branch were two birds. There are four children in my family. Here is my friend.
- Many questions are in inverted order.   EXAMPLE: Where is Jim?
- Sometimes the subject of a sentence is not expressed, as in a command or request. The understood subject is you.   EXAMPLES: Bring the sandwiches. (You) bring the sandwiches.

- **Rewrite each inverted sentence in natural order. Rewrite commands or requests by including you as the subject. Then underline each simple subject once and each simple predicate twice in each sentence you write.**

1. Where was the sunken treasure ship?

   The sunken treasure ship was where?
   _____

2. Beyond the bridge were several sailboats.

   _____

3. There is no one in that room.

   _____

4. From the gymnasium came the shouts of the victorious team.

   _____

5. Beside the walk grew beautiful flowers.

   _____

6. When is the surprise party?

   _____

7. Bring your sales report to the meeting.

   _____

8. There were only three floats in the parade.

   _____

9. From the yard came the bark of a dog.

   _____

10. Place the forks to the left of the plate.

    _____

Compound Subjects

> ■ A **compound subject** is made up of two or more simple subjects.
> EXAMPLE: **Henri** and **Tanya** / are tall people.

A. Draw a line between the complete subject and the complete predicate in each sentence. Write SS for a simple subject. Write CS for a compound subject.

__CS__   **1.** Arturo and I / often work late on Friday.

_____   **2.** Sandy left the person near the crowded exit.

_____   **3.** She and I will mail the packages to Invermere, B.C., today.

_____   **4.** Shanghai and New Delhi are two cities visited by the group.

_____   **5.** The fire spread rapidly to other buildings in the neighbourhood.

_____   **6.** Laszlo and Lenora helped their parents with the chores.

_____   **7.** Swimming, jogging, and hiking were our favourite sports.

_____   **8.** Melbourne and Sydney are important Australian cities.

_____   **9.** Eric and I had an interesting experience Saturday.

_____   **10.** The Red Sea and the Mediterranean Sea are connected by the Suez Canal.

_____   **11.** The Conservatives, the Liberals, and the New Democrats made many promises.

_____   **12.** The people waved to us from the top of the cliff.

_____   **13.** Liz and Tran crated the freshly-picked apples.

_____   **14.** Clean clothes and a neat appearance are important in an interview.

_____   **15.** The kitten and the old dog are good friends.

_____   **16.** David and Paul are on their way to the swimming pool.

_____   **17.** Tom combed his dog's shiny black coat.

_____   **18.** Redbud and dogwood trees bloom in the spring.

_____   **19.** I hummed a cheerful tune on the way to the meeting.

_____   **20.** Buffalo, deer, and antelope once roamed the plains of North America.

_____   **21.** Gina and Hiroshi raked the leaves.

_____   **22.** Brasília and São Paulo are two cities in Brazil.

_____   **23.** Hang gliding is a popular sport in Hawaii.

_____   **24.** Our class went on a field trip to the aquarium.

_____   **25.** The doctor asked him to get a blood test.

B. Write two sentences containing compound subjects.

1. _____

2. _____

Compound Predicates

> ▪ A **compound predicate** is made up of two or more simple predicates.
>   EXAMPLE: Joseph/**dances** and **sings**.

A. Draw a line between the complete subject and the complete predicate in each sentence. Write <u>SP</u> for each simple predicate. Write <u>CP</u> for each compound predicate.

<u> CP </u> **1.** Edward / grinned and nodded.

_____ **2.** Plants need air to live.

_____ **3.** Old silver tea kettles were among their possessions.

_____ **4.** My sister buys and sells real estate.

_____ **5.** Snow covered every highway in the area.

_____ **6.** Mr. Sanders designs and makes odd pieces of furniture.

_____ **7.** Popcorn is one of my favourite snack foods.

_____ **8.** Soccer is one of my favourite sports.

_____ **9.** The ducks quickly crossed the road and found the ducklings.

_____ **10.** They came early and stayed late.

_____ **11.** Crystal participated in the Special Olympics this year.

_____ **12.** Massoud raked and sacked the leaves.

_____ **13.** Perry built the fire and cooked supper.

_____ **14.** We collected old newspapers for the recycling centre.

_____ **15.** Doug arrived in Toronto, Ontario, during the afternoon.

_____ **16.** Tony's parents are visiting in New Brunswick and Nova Scotia.

_____ **17.** The Pavels live in that apartment building on Oak Street.

_____ **18.** The shingles were picked up and delivered today.

_____ **19.** The audience talked and laughed before the performance.

_____ **20.** Automobiles crowd and jam that highway early in the morning.

_____ **21.** The apples are rotting in the boxes.

_____ **22.** The leader of the group grumbled and scolded.

_____ **23.** She worked hard and waited patiently.

_____ **24.** Nelson Mandela is a great civil rights activist.

_____ **25.** The supervisor has completed the work for the week.

B. Write two sentences containing compound predicates.

1. _____

2. _____

                     Unit 2, Sentences

Combining Sentences

- Two sentences in which the subjects are different and the predicates are the same can be combined into one sentence. The two subjects are joined by <u>and</u>.
    EXAMPLE: **Hurricanes** are storms. **Tornadoes** are storms.
    Hurricanes and tornadoes are storms.
- Two sentences in which the subjects are the same and the predicates are different can be combined into one sentence. The two predicates may be joined by <u>or</u>, <u>and</u>, or <u>but</u>.
    EXAMPLE: Hurricanes **begin over tropical oceans**. Hurricanes **move inland**. Hurricanes **begin over tropical oceans and move inland**.

- **Combine each pair of sentences below. Underline the compound subject or the compound predicate in each sentence that you write.**

1. Lightning is part of a thunderstorm. Thunder is part of a thunderstorm.

   _____

2. Thunderstorms usually happen in the spring. Thunderstorms bring heavy rains.

   _____

3. Depending on how close or far away it is, thunder sounds like a sharp crack. Depending on how close or far away it is, thunder rumbles.

   _____

   _____

4. Lightning is very exciting to watch. Lightning can be very dangerous.

   _____

5. Lightning causes many fires. Lightning harms many people.

   _____

6. An open field is an unsafe place to be during a thunderstorm. A golf course is an unsafe place to be during a thunderstorm.

   _____

   _____

7. During a thunderstorm, my dog gets scared. During a thunderstorm, my dog hides under the bed.

   _____

   _____

8. A lightning rod is a metal rod placed on the top of a building. A lightning rod is connected to the ground by a cable.

   _____

   _____

> - The **direct object** tells who or what receives the action of the verb. The direct object is a noun or pronoun that follows an action verb.
>
> EXAMPLE: You told the **truth**.
> DO

- **Underline the verb in each sentence. Then write <u>DO</u> above each direct object.**

1. Elephants <u>can carry</u> logs with their trunks.
   (DO above "logs")

2. Who made this magazine rack?

3. Do you always plan a daily schedule?

4. They easily won the game.

5. Martin baked an apple pie for dinner.

6. Who tuned your piano?

7. I take guitar lessons once a week.

8. Who composed this melody?

9. I especially enjoy mystery stories.

10. The astronauts orbited the earth many times.

11. I bought this coat in Vancouver.

12. Did he find his glasses?

13. Zoe drove the truck to the hardware store.

14. The boy shrugged his shoulders.

15. We have finished our work today.

16. We drink milk with breakfast.

17. She can solve any problem quickly.

18. Who made your wreath?

19. You will learn something from this lesson.

20. Every person needs friends.

21. I have found a dime.

22. Yuko ate an apple for a snack.

> - The **indirect object** is the noun or pronoun that tells to whom or for whom an action is done. In order to have an indirect object, a sentence must have a direct object.
> - The indirect object is usually placed between the action verb and the direct object.
>
>   IO   DO
>   EXAMPLE: Who sold **you** that fantastic **bike**?

- **Underline the verb in each sentence. Then write <u>DO</u> above the direct object and <u>IO</u> above the indirect object.**

                          IO   DO

1. Certain marine plants <u>give</u> the Red Sea its colour.

2. I gave the cashier a cheque for twenty dollars.

3. The magician showed the audience a few of her tricks.

4. The coach taught them the rules of the game.

5. Roberto brought us some foreign coins.

6. This interesting book will give every reader pleasure.

7. Have you written your brother a letter?

8. They made us some sandwiches to take on our hike.

9. The astronaut gave Mission Control the data.

10. I bought my friend an etching at the art exhibit.

11. James, did you sell Mike your car?

12. We have given the dog a thorough scrubbing.

13. Give the usher your ticket.

14. Carl brought my brother a gold ring from Mexico.

15. Hand me a pencil, please.

16. The conductor gave the orchestra a short break.

17. Show me the picture of your boat.

18. I have given you my money.

19. Give Leo this message.

20. The club gave the town a new statue.

Lesson 20

Independent and Subordinate Clauses

> - A **clause** is a group of words that contains a subject and a predicate. There are two kinds of clauses: **independent clauses** and **subordinate clauses**.
> - An **independent clause** can stand alone as a sentence because it expresses a complete thought.
>   EXAMPLE: **The students came** in when the bell rang.
>   **The students came in.**

A. Underline the independent clause in each sentence below.

1. Frank will be busy because he is studying.

2. I have only one hour that I can spare.

3. The project must be finished when I get back.

4. Gloria volunteered to do the typing that needs to be done.

5. The work is going too slowly for us to finish on time.

6. Before Nathan started to help, I didn't think we could finish.

7. What else should we do before we relax?

8. Since you forgot to give this page to Gloria, you can type it.

9. After she had finished typing, we completed the project.

10. We actually got it finished before the deadline.

> - A **subordinate clause** has a subject and predicate but cannot stand alone as a sentence because it does not express a complete thought. A subordinate clause must be combined with an independent clause to make a sentence.
>   EXAMPLE: The stamp **that I bought** was already in my collection.

B. Underline the subordinate clause in each sentence below.

1. The people who went shopping found a great sale.

2. Tony's bike, which is a mountain bike, came from that store.

3. Juana was sad when the sale was over.

4. Marianne was excited because she wanted some new things.

5. Thomas didn't find anything since he went late.

6. The mall where we went shopping was new.

7. The people who own the stores are proud of the beautiful setting.

8. The mall, which is far away, is serviced by the city bus.

9. We ran as fast as we could because the bus was coming.

10. We were panting because we had run fast.

     Unit 2, Sentences

> ■ An **adjective clause** is a subordinate clause that modifies a noun or a
> pronoun. It answers the adjective question <u>Which one</u>? or <u>What kind</u>? It
> usually modifies the word directly preceding it. Most adjective clauses
> begin with a **relative pronoun**. A relative pronoun relates an adjective
> clause to the noun or pronoun that the clause modifies. <u>Who</u>, <u>whose</u>,
> <u>which</u>, and <u>that</u> are relative pronouns.
>   EXAMPLE: The coat **that I bought** was on sale.
>   noun   adjective clause

A. Underline the adjective clause in each sentence below.

1. A compass has a needle that always points northward.

2. A seismograph is an instrument that measures earthquake tremors.

3. People who work in science laboratories today have a broad field of study.

4. This will be the first time that she has played in that position.

5. Jay is the person whose wrist was broken.

6. The fish that I caught was large.

7. A sentence that contains a subordinate clause is a complex sentence.

8. Here is the photograph that I promised to show you.

9. The book that I read was very humorous.

B. Add an adjective clause to each independent clause below.

1. A microscope is an instrument   (that) _____

   _____

2. Amelia Earhart was a pilot   (who) _____

   _____

3. We have football players   (who) _____

   _____

4. We had strawberries for dessert,   (which) _____

   _____

5. Bunny is a dog   (that) _____

   _____

6. A telescope is an instrument   (that) _____

   _____

Adverb Clauses

> ■ An **adverb clause** is a subordinate clause that modifies a verb, an adjective, or another adverb. It answers the adverb question <u>How</u>? <u>Under what condition</u>? or <u>Why</u>? Words that introduce adverb clauses are called **subordinating conjunctions**. The many subordinating conjunctions include such words as <u>when</u>, <u>after</u>, <u>before</u>, <u>since</u>, <u>although</u>, and <u>because</u>.
>
> EXAMPLE: I finished **before the bell rang**.
> adverb clause

A. Underline the adverb clause in each sentence below.

1. We had agreed to go hiking when the cloudy skies cleared.

2. Although the weather was mild and sunny, we took along our jackets.

3. Clouds began to move in once again after we arrived at the park.

4. We felt comfortable about the weather because we were prepared.

5. Since we had our jackets, we didn't get too cold.

6. Although the clouds remained, it never rained.

7. It was exhilarating to see the view when we got to the top of the hill.

8. After enjoying the beauty and the quiet for a while, we hiked back down.

9. We decided to drive home the long way since it was still early.

10. We had a wonderful day because we were so relaxed and happy.

B. Add an adverb clause to each independent clause below.

1. We ate breakfast   (before) _____

_____

2. Jay and I carried umbrellas   (since) _____

_____

3. We took the bus to the museum   (because) _____

_____

4. People in line waited   (when) _____

_____

5. We saw the exhibit   (after) _____

_____

6. Joel and I baked cookies   (when) _____

_____

Simple and Compound Sentences

> - A **simple sentence** contains only one independent clause. The subject, the predicate, or both may be compound.
>   EXAMPLES: The courthouse/is the oldest building in town. Gale and Louise/are making costumes and dressing up.
> - A **compound sentence** consists of two or more independent clauses. Each independent clause in a compound sentence can stand alone as a separate sentence. The independent clauses are usually joined by <u>and</u>, <u>but</u>, <u>so</u>, <u>or</u>, <u>for</u>, or <u>yet</u> and a comma.
>   EXAMPLE: Jack brought the chairs, but Mary forgot the extra table.
> - Sometimes a **semicolon** (;) is used to join two independent clauses in a compound sentence.
>   EXAMPLE: The music started; the dance had begun.

A. Write <u>S</u> before each simple sentence, and write <u>CS</u> before each compound sentence.

_____ **1.** We can wait for Jesper, or we can go on ahead.

_____ **2.** The carnival will start today in the empty lot.

_____ **3.** Jack and Manuel are going to meet us there at six o'clock.

_____ **4.** I really want to go to the carnival, yet I am not sure about going tonight.

_____ **5.** I didn't mean to hurt Carl's feelings by not going.

_____ **6.** You wait for the package, and I'll meet you at the carnival.

_____ **7.** I can't skip my homework to go, but maybe I'll finish it this afternoon.

_____ **8.** Jan and Alicia are both working at the carnival this year.

B. Put brackets ([ ]) around the independent clauses in each compound sentence. Then underline the word or punctuation used to join the clauses.

1. You must observe all the rules, or you must withdraw from the race.

2. I did well on the test, and Rita did well, too.

3. Shall I carry this box, or do you want to leave it here?

4. Put the key in your pocket, or it may get lost.

5. He threw a beautiful pass, but no one caught it.

6. The doctor treated the cut, but he did not have to make any stitches.

7. I like to spend weekends at home, but the others prefer to travel.

8. The year is almost over, and everyone is thinking of the new year.

9. The family faced every hardship, yet they were thankful for what they had.

10. Move the box over here; I'll unpack it.

11. Connie likes football; James prefers hockey.

12. I drive safely, but I always make everyone fasten their seat belts.

13. Please get the telephone number, and I'll call after work.

> ▪ A **complex sentence** contains one independent clause and one or more
> subordinate clauses.
>   EXAMPLE: The person **who helps me carry these** gets some dessert.
>   subordinate clause

A. **Put brackets around the subordinate clause, and underline the independent clause in each complex sentence below.**

1. <u>The shadows</u> [that had fallen between the trees] <u>were a deep purple</u>.

2. The soldiers waded across the stream where the water was shallow.

3. They waited for me until the last bus came.

4. The fans of that team were sad when the team lost the game.

5. When George was here, he was charmed by the beauty of the hills.

6. Sophia will call for you when she is ready.

7. Some spiders that are found in Sumatra have legs forty centimetres long.

8. Those who are going will arrive on time.

9. Do not throw the bat after you've hit the ball.

10. Tell us about the trip that you made a year ago.

B. **Add a subordinate clause that begins with the word in parentheses to make a complex sentence.**

1. I try not to drive   (where) _____

_____

2. The electric light is an important invention   (that) _____

_____

3. The telephone stopped ringing   (before) _____

_____

4. He is the man   (who) _____

_____

5. This is the book   (that) _____

_____

6. Turn to the left   (when) _____

_____

Correcting Run-on Sentences

> - Two or more independent clauses that are run together without the correct punctuation are called a **run-on sentence**.
>   EXAMPLE: The music was deafening I turned down the volume.
> - One way to correct a run-on sentence is to separate it into two sentences.
>   EXAMPLE: The music was deafening. I turned down the volume.
> - Another way to correct a run-on sentence is to make it into a compound sentence.
>   EXAMPLE: The music was deafening, so I turned down the volume.
> - Another way to correct a run-on sentence is to use a semicolon.
>   EXAMPLE: The music was deafening; I turned down the volume.

- **Correct each run-on sentence below by writing it as two sentences or as a compound sentence.**

1. The city council held a meeting a meeting is held every month.

_____

_____

2. The council members are elected by the voters there are two thousand voters in the city.

_____

_____

3. There is one council member from each suburb, the president is elected by the council members.

_____

_____

4. Those who run for office must give speeches, the speeches should be short.

_____

_____

5. The council decides on many activities every activity is voted on.

_____

_____

6. Money is needed for many of the special activities, the council also plans fund-raisers in the city.

_____

_____

7. The annual city picnic is sponsored by the city council the picnic is in June.

_____

_____

26

Expanding Sentences

> - Sentences can be **expanded** by adding details to make them clearer and more interesting.
>   EXAMPLE: The audience laughed. The **excited** audience **in the theatre** laughed **loudly**.
> - Details added to sentences may answer these questions: When? Where? How? How often? To what degree? What kind? Which? How many?

A. Expand each sentence below by adding details to answer the questions shown in parentheses. Write the expanded sentence on the line.

1. The car stalled.   (What kind? Where?)

   _____

2. Mary raised the hood.   (How? Which?)

   _____

3. Smoke billowed from the engine.   (What kind? Where?)

   _____

4. She called the service station.   (When? Which?)

   _____

5. The phone rang.   (Which? How often?)

   _____

B. Decide how each of the following sentences can be expanded. Write your expanded sentence on the line.

1. The runner crossed the finish line.

   _____

2. The crowd cheered.

   _____

3. The reporter interviewed her.

   _____

4. She answered.

   _____

5. Her coach ran up to her.

   _____

6. She and her coach walked off the track.

   _____

7. She was awarded the medal.

   _____

Review

A. Label each sentence as follows: Write **D** for declarative, **IN** for interrogative, **IM** for imperative, or **E** for exclamatory. Write **X** if it is not a sentence. Punctuate each sentence correctly.

_____ 1. Did you forget our appointment _____

_____ 2. Be careful _____

_____ 3. Rolled up our sleeping bags _____

_____ 4. All members will meet in this room _____

_____ 5. Help, I'm frightened _____

_____ 6. Where are you going _____

_____ 7. Oh, look out _____

_____ 8. People from all over the world _____

_____ 9. Julie ran three kilometres _____

_____ 10. Place the books here _____

B. In each sentence below, underline the words that are identified in parentheses.

1. (complete subject)   The lights around the public square went out.

2. (simple subject)   Stations are in all parts of our country.

3. (direct object)   Carmen collects fans for a hobby.

4. (complete predicate)   We drove slowly across the bridge.

5. (simple predicate)   We saw an unusual flower.

6. (compound predicate)   Taro swims and dives quite well.

7. (compound subject)   The cake and bread are kept in the box.

8. (indirect object)   The referee gave our team a penalty.

9. (direct object)   A good citizen obeys the laws.

10. (indirect object)   Please lend me your raincoat, so I can stay dry.

C. Write **CP** after each compound sentence and **CX** after each complex sentence.

1. The food that is needed will be bought. _____

2. Beatrice will get lettuce, but we may have some. _____

3. Jack, who said he would help, is late. _____

4. We will go, and they will meet us. _____

5. Jack will drive his car after it has been repaired. _____

6. We are going to Spruce Park since it is on a lake. _____

7. There are canoes that can be rented. _____

8. We can row around the lake, or we can go swimming. _____

9. We can decide what we want to do after we eat our picnic lunch. _____

10. Spruce Park is a great place, and we are going to have a wonderful time. _____

D. Underline the verb in each sentence. Then write <u>DO</u> above the direct object and <u>IO</u> above the indirect object.

1. The director gave the actors a new script.

2. Jenny showed her friends her vacation slides.

3. Ms. Lopez took her sick neighbour some chicken soup.

4. We handed the cashier our money.

5. Enrique, please give your brother his jacket.

E. Underline the independent clause, and circle the subordinate clause in each sentence.

1. The campers got wet when it started raining.

2. The candidates that I voted for in the election won easily.

3. Before the board voted on the issue, it held public hearings.

4. The freeway through town is a road where vehicles often speed.

5. While we waited, the children kept us entertained.

F. Underline the subordinate clause in each sentence. Write <u>adjective clause</u> or <u>adverb clause</u> on the line after each sentence.

1. Meteorologists are people who are trained in weather forecasting. _____

2. Before I decided on a university, I did many hours of research. _____

3. The experiment that I designed failed completely. _____

4. Although the furniture was old, it was very comfortable. _____

5. Many people exercise because they want to stay healthy. _____

6. I ate breakfast before I left. _____

G. Rewrite each sentence in natural order.

1. Just below the surface lay a large goldfish.

_____

2. Over the roof flew the baseball.

_____

H. Combine each pair of sentences to form a compound sentence.

1. Dogs are Erica's favourite animal. Cats are John's favourite animal.

_____

2. The water reflected the sun. We put on our sunglasses.

_____

 Unit 2, Sentences

A. Read the sentences in the box. Then answer the questions below.

> **A.** Did I give you the tickets for the show?
> **B.** This compact disc is fantastic!
> **C.** Be at my house by seven o'clock.
> **D.** You and I can ride downtown together.
> **E.** We can stop and eat before the show.

1. _____ Which sentence has a compound subject?
2. _____ Which sentence has a compound predicate?
3. _____ Which sentence has a direct object?
4. _____ Which sentence has an indirect object?

5. _____ Which sentence is interrogative?
6. _____ Which sentences are declarative?
7. _____ Which sentence is exclamatory?
8. _____ Which sentence is imperative?

9. What is the complete subject of E? _____

10. What is the simple subject of E? _____

11. What is the complete predicate of C? _____

B. Underline the independent clause, and circle the subordinate clause in each complex sentence below.

1. The streamers sagged after we hung them.

2. Mark knows party planning because he has many parties.

3. Everyone who wants to go to the party must bring something.

4. If everyone brings something, the party will be great.

5. Unless I am wrong, the party is tomorrow.

6. As if everything had been done, Jake ran out of the room.

7. The girls who planned the party received roses.

8. I will never forget the day that I fell on my face at a party.

C. Combine each pair of sentences below to form a compound sentence.

1. The team sat in the dugout. The fans sat in the stands.

_____

2. The rain finally stopped. The game continued.

_____

3. It was the bottom of the ninth inning. There were two outs.

_____

4. The batter swung at the pitch. The umpire called, "Strike three!"

_____

D. Rewrite each inverted sentence in natural order.

1. On the rocks perched two seagulls.

_____

2. Here are the supplies for the office.

_____

E. Create complex sentences by adding a subordinate clause or an independent clause to each group of words below.

1. He turned down the lonely road _____

2. When night came, _____

3. This was the site _____

4. After he looked around, _____

5. He continued to drive _____

6. When he got to the inn, _____

F. Rewrite the paragraph below, correcting the run-on sentences.

   Patricia didn't know what to do, she had a terrible problem and she was trying to solve it. No matter how hard she thought about it no answers seemed to come. She decided to take a break and not think about it for a while. She went to the mall where she always enjoyed browsing in the bookstore she wasn't even thinking about the problem, the answer just popped into her head she was so excited about solving her problem she completely forgot about the bookstore.

_____

_____

_____

_____

_____

_____

G. Read the two sentences below. Then expand each sentence by adding details to make the sentences clearer and more interesting.

The tree crashed. Everyone screamed.

_____

_____

Lesson 27

Nouns

> ■ A **noun** is a word that names a person, place, thing, or quality.
> EXAMPLE: Nancy Fisher is my friend.

■ **Circle the nouns in each sentence.**

1. Mariko Tanaka has worked here for years and is now a supervisor.

2. The triangular piece of land at the mouth of a river is called a delta.

3. Yousuf Karsh, a Canadian photographer, has photographed many celebrities.

4. Albert Einstein, the greatest scientist of our century, was born in Germany.

5. The greatest library of the ancient world was in Alexandria, Egypt.

6. Donovan Bailey, of Oakville, Ontario, is among the greatest athletes in the world.

7. Bryan Adams is the most successful Canadian rock star ever.

8. Marconi invented the wireless telegraph.

9. Do you watch the parades and football games on television on New Year's Day?

10. Terry Fox, a runner who lost a leg to cancer, ran 5342 kilometres across Canada.

11. The *Halifax Gazette* was the first newspaper in Canada.

12. The first wireless message was sent across the English Channel in the nineteenth century.

13. Chicoutimi is a city on the Saguenay River.

14. His seat is by the window.

15. Kuang likes his new car.

16. They have promised their children a trip to Canada's Wonderland.

17. Superb is a town in the province of Saskatchewan.

18. France grows more food than any other country in Western Europe.

19. Tania was excited about her new job.

20. Hailstones are frozen raindrops, but snowflakes are not.

21. The days are usually warm in the summer.

22. Many rivers were named by explorers.

23. Geoff built a carport to store his boat.

24. California is home to many movie stars.

25. William Caxton printed the first book in England.

26. Chris bought tomatoes, lettuce, and cherries at the market.

27. That building has offices, stores, and apartments.

28. Leticia drove to Pushthrough, Newfoundland, to see her friend.

29. The airport was closed for five hours due to a snowstorm.

30. My pen is almost out of ink.

Common and Proper Nouns

> - There are two main classes of nouns: **common nouns** and **proper nouns**.
> - A **common noun** names any one of a class of objects.
>   EXAMPLES: child, tree, home
> - A **proper noun** names a particular person, place, or thing. It begins with a capital letter.
>   EXAMPLES: Margaret Laurence, Chilliwack, House of Commons

A. Underline the common nouns, and circle the proper nouns in each sentence.

1. In the story, a prince and a pauper changed clothing.

2. Estevan, Saskatchewan is close to the border between Canada and the United States.

3. Do you remember the story about Scrooge and Tiny Tim?

4. Sumatra is a large island in the Indian Ocean.

5. In Canada, the weather is a favourite topic of conversation.

6. We learned to make paper from the Chinese.

7. "Rikki-tikki-tavi," by Rudyard Kipling, is a story about a mongoose.

8. *Shamrock* is the name commonly given to the national emblem of Ireland.

9. The shilling is a silver coin used in England.

10. The lights of our car were reflected in the wet pavement.

11. Nathan, did you come with Sam last Tuesday?

12. The Great Sphinx is the most famous monument in Egypt.

13. My family visited Mexico and Guatemala this year.

B. Write a common noun suggested by each proper noun.

1. Panama _____
2. Treasure Island _____
3. Linda _____
4. Alberta _____
5. Beethoven _____
6. Pacific _____
7. Iceland _____
8. Saturn _____
9. Ms. Taylor _____
10. Africa _____
11. Edison _____
12. North America _____
13. December _____
14. Toronto _____
15. University of Ottawa _____
16. Rocky Mountains _____
17. Dr. Dean _____
18. Huron _____
19. Tuesday _____
20. Thanksgiving _____

C. Write a proper noun suggested by each common noun.

1. continent _____
2. mountain _____
3. hotel _____
4. hero _____
5. inventor _____
6. building _____
7. day _____
8. physician _____
9. holiday _____
10. province _____

11. actor _____
12. magazine _____
13. month _____
14. lake _____
15. school _____
16. river _____
17. song _____
18. premier _____
19. explorer _____
20. basketball team _____

D. Write a sentence in which you use a proper noun suggested to you by each phrase.

1. Your province _____

_____

2. Name of a foreign country _____

_____

3. Name of a singer _____

_____

4. Name of the make of an automobile _____

_____

5. Name of a store near your home _____

_____

6. Name of a television star _____

_____

7. Name of an ocean _____

_____

8. Name of the Prime Minister of Canada _____

_____

The following chart shows how to change **singular nouns** into **plural nouns**.

Noun	Plural Form	Examples
Most nouns	Add -s	ship, ships nose, noses
Nouns ending in a consonant and -y	Change the -y to -i, and add -es	sky, skies navy, navies
Nouns ending in -o	Add -s or -es	hero, heroes piano, pianos
Most nouns ending in -f or -fe	Change the -f or -fe to -ves	half, halves
Most nouns ending in -ch, -sh, -s, or -x	Add -es	bench, benches bush, bushes tax, taxes
Many two-word or three-word compound nouns	Add -s to the principle word	son-in-law, sons-in-law
Nouns with the same form in the singular and plural	No change	sheep

A. Fill in the blank with the plural form of the word in parentheses.

1. (brush)   These are plastic _____ .

2. (lunch)   That café on the corner serves well-balanced _____ .

3. (country)   What _____ belong to the United Nations?

4. (bench)   There are many iron _____ in the park.

5. (earring)   These _____ came from Italy.

6. (calf)   How many _____ are in that pen?

7. (piano)   There are three _____ in the warehouse.

8. (fox)   Did you see the _____ at the zoo?

9. (daisy)   We bought Susan a bunch of _____ .

10. (potato)   Do you like baked _____ ?

11. (dish)   Please help wash the _____ .

12. (store)   There are three _____ near my house.

B. Write the correct plural form for each singular noun.

1. booklet _____
2. tomato _____
3. truck _____
4. chef _____
5. branch _____
6. toddler _____
7. penny _____
8. potato _____
9. piece _____
10. door _____
11. island _____
12. country _____
13. house _____
14. garage _____
15. fish _____

16. watch _____
17. elf _____
18. desk _____
19. pan _____
20. sheep _____
21. garden _____
22. pony _____
23. solo _____
24. tree _____
25. light _____
26. church _____
27. city _____
28. spoonful _____
29. vacation _____
30. home _____

C. Rewrite the sentences, changing each underlined singular noun to a plural noun.

1. Put the apple and orange in the box.

_____

2. Jan wrote five letter to her friend.

_____

3. Those building each have four elevator.

_____

4. Our family drove many kilometre to get to the lake.

_____

5. The top of those car were damaged in the storm.

_____

6. My aunt and uncle attended the family reunion.

_____

- A **possessive noun** shows possession of the noun that follows.
- Form the possessive of most singular nouns by adding an apostrophe (') and -s.   EXAMPLES: a child's toy, my teacher's classroom
- Form the possessive of plural nouns ending in -s by adding only an apostrophe.   EXAMPLES: our books' pages, those stores' windows
- Form the possessive of plural nouns that do not end in -s by adding an apostrophe and -s.   EXAMPLES: some women's clothes, many men's shoes

A. Write the possessive form of each noun.

1. brother _____

2. boy _____

3. Carol _____

4. children _____

5. grandmother _____

6. men _____

7. heroes _____

8. women _____

9. ox _____

10. man _____

11. Dr. Kahn _____

12. soldier _____

13. pony _____

14. friend _____

15. child _____

16. engineers _____

17. birds _____

18. Jon _____

B. Write ten sentences using possessive nouns formed in Exercise A.

1. _____

2. _____

3. _____

4. _____

5. _____

6. _____

7. _____

8. _____

9. _____

10. _____

C. Complete each sentence with the possessive form of the word in parentheses.

1. (doctor)   My _____ office is closed.

2. (lecturer)   The _____ speech was astounding.

3. (sheep)   What is the old saying about a wolf in _____ clothing?

4. (baby)   Are the _____ hands cold?

5. (instructor)   My _____ classroom is on this floor.

6. (collectors)   Let's form a _____ club.

7. (spider)   A _____ web has a complicated design.

8. (Mr. Takata)   _____ store was damaged by the flood.

9. (Tim)   _____ brother found this purse.

10. (Beth)   _____ business is successful.

11. (Dennis Lee)   _____ poems are enjoyed by people of all ages.

12. (child)   The _____ book is torn.

13. (women)   That store sells _____ clothing.

14. (elephants)   There were seats on the _____ backs.

15. (sister)   My _____ room is at the front of the house.

16. (Brazil)   What is the name of _____ largest river?

17. (friends)   Those are my _____ homes.

18. (bird)   That _____ nest is very close to the ground.

19. (children)   The library has a table of _____ books.

20. (owl)   I heard an _____ hoot during the night.

21. (brothers)   Please get your _____ shirts from the dryer.

22. (student)   The _____ pen ran out of ink.

23. (country)   They played that _____ national anthem.

24. (owner)   The dog lay at its _____ feet.

25. (uncle)   I visited my _____ laundry.

26. (Joan)   _____ paintings sell well.

27. (men)   The _____ jackets are brown.

- An **appositive** is a noun that identifies or explains the noun or pronoun it follows.
  - EXAMPLE: My dog, **Fido**, won a medal.
- An **appositive phrase** consists of an appositive and its modifiers.
  - EXAMPLE: My book, **a novel set in Newfoundland**, is one of the best I've read.
- Use **commas** to set off an appositive or an appositive phrase that is not essential to the meaning of the sentence.
  - EXAMPLE: William Gray, my uncle, owns that home.
- Don't use commas if the appositive is essential to the meaning of the sentence.
  - EXAMPLES: My brother Kevin arrived late. My other brother Charlie arrived early.

A. Underline the appositive or appositive phrase, and circle the noun that it identifies.

1. Prince Edward Island, Canada's smallest province, is my favourite place to visit.

2. The painter Vincent Van Gogh cut off part of his ear.

3. Twenty-four Sussex Drive, the home of the Prime Minister of Canada, is closed to the public.

4. Uncle Marco, my mother's brother, is an engineer.

5. Earth, the only inhabited planet in our solar system, is home to a diverse population of plants and animals.

6. The scorpion, a native of the southwestern part of North America, has a poisonous sting.

7. Emily's prize Persian cat Amelia won first prize at the cat show.

8. Judge Andropov, the presiding judge, sentenced the criminal to prison.

9. Paula's friend from South Africa, Elynor, came to visit her.

B. Complete each sentence with an appropriate appositive.

1. My friend _____ bought a new bike.

2. The bike, _____ , is fast and sleek.

3. Joe and his friend _____ plan to ride their bikes together.

4. They will ride to Brock Park, _____ , on Saturday.

5. They plan to meet Eva, _____ , on the bike path.

6. After bicycling, they will see a movie, _____ .

7. Our friend _____ might come with us.

8. We will get a snack, _____ , to eat during the movie.

9. My favourite actor, _____ , might be in the movie.

Lesson 32

Action Verbs

- A **verb** is a word that expresses action, being, or state of being.
  EXAMPLE: Paul **went** to the store.
- An **action verb** is a verb that expresses action.
  EXAMPLE: The track star **ran** fast.

- **Underline the action verb in each sentence.**

1. Watch your favourite television program.
2. Andrea carefully dusted her new piano.
3. Sasha, copy the pages carefully.
4. A wood fire burned in the huge fireplace.
5. This button fell from my sweater.
6. The Harlem Globe Trotters play basketball throughout the world.
7. The musicians practised for the concert.
8. The waves dashed the light craft against the rocks.
9. A sentence expresses a complete thought.
10. Everybody enjoys a good laugh.
11. This long, narrow trail leads to the mountaintop.
12. It snowed almost every day in February.
13. We hiked along the Bruce Trail.
14. Dan made me a delicious sandwich.
15. Please hand me the salt, Charlotte.
16. Draw a line under each verb.
17. We skated on Lake Superior.
18. The woman answered all my questions.
19. The city repaired that pothole last week.
20. Early settlers suffered many hardships.
21. Write your sentence on the board.
22. They moved the car from the street.
23. Thomas Edison often worked eighteen hours a day.
24. Pamira directs the community choir.
25. The team played softball all afternoon.
26. We walked along the beach for an hour.
27. Who helped you with your science project?
28. The bridge collapsed.
29. The antique clock ticked loudly.

33 Linking Verbs

> ■ A **linking verb** does not show action. Instead, it links the subject to a word that either describes the subject or gives the subject another name.
> ■ A verb is a linking verb if it can replace one of the verbs of being (<u>am</u>, <u>is</u>, <u>are</u>, <u>was</u>, <u>were</u>).
>   EXAMPLES: We **were** cold. Nancy **is** a dancer. John **looked** tired. The soup **tastes** delicious.

A. Underline the linking verb in each sentence.

1. Marta appears nervous.

2. She is the first singer on the program.

3. Last year, she was last on the program.

4. Another performer is last this year.

5. The stage looks beautiful.

6. Flowers are everywhere.

7. The flowers smell fresh.

8. Marta feels ready to start.

9. Her song sounds wonderful.

10. The audience seems pleased.

B. Complete each sentence with a linking verb from the box. You may use any verb more than once.

am	appeared	are	became	is	seemed	was	were

1. Tony _____ frightened.

2. He _____ alone in the cabin for the first time.

3. In the dark forest, everything _____ threatening.

4. Because of the storm, the lights _____ out.

5. Even the shadows _____ strange.

6. "This _____ stupid," he thought to himself.

7. "I _____ brave; I'm not a coward."

8. "Where _____ Aaron?" he wondered.

9. There _____ bears in the woods.

10. What if he _____ lost?

 Unit 3, Grammar and Usage

- A verb has four principal parts: **present**, **present participle**, **past**, and **past participle**.
- For regular verbs, form the present participle by adding <u>-ing</u> to the present. Use a form of the helping verb <u>be</u> with the present participle.
- Form the past and past participle by adding <u>-ed</u> to the present. Use a form of the helping verb <u>have</u> with the past participle.

  EXAMPLES:

<u>Present</u>	<u>Present Participle</u>	<u>Past</u>	<u>Past Participle</u>
laugh	(is) laughing	laughed	(have, has, had) laughed
bake	(is) baking	baked	(have, has, had) baked
live	(is) living	lived	(have, has, had) lived

- Irregular verbs form their past and past participle in other ways. A dictionary shows the principal parts of these verbs.

- **Write the present participle, past, and past participle for each verb.**

PRESENT	PRESENT PARTICIPLE	PAST	PAST PARTICIPLE
1. stop	is stopping	stopped	(have, has, had) stopped
2. listen			
3. carry			
4. help			
5. start			
6. borrow			
7. call			
8. receive			
9. hope			
10. illustrate			
11. divide			
12. change			
13. score			
14. iron			
15. study			
16. collect			
17. laugh			

- A **verb phrase** consists of a main verb and one or more **helping verbs**. A helping verb is also called an **auxiliary verb**. In a verb phrase, the helping verb or verbs precede the main verb.   EXAMPLE: Peter **has arrived**.
- The helping verbs are:
    am, are, is, was, were, be, being, been
    has, have, had
    do, does, did
    can, could, must, may, might, shall, should, will, would

A. Write a sentence using each word below as the main verb in a verb phrase.

1. gone _____

2. written _____

3. come _____

4. thrown _____

5. draw _____

6. walking _____

7. invent _____

8. sing _____

9. seen _____

10. eaten _____

B. Underline the verb phrase in each sentence.

1. Isabel has returned from a vacation in Cuba.

2. She has planned to tell us all about it.

3. Isabel would have answered every question about her trip.

4. Our club officers have been looking for someone to speak.

5. The officers have asked Isabel to the meeting.

6. They have organized an interesting meeting.

7. Every detail of the meeting has been planned carefully.

8. I must speak to Isabel immediately.

9. The lights were dimmed for Isabel's slide show.

10. She said that alligators had been seen in some places.

11. Pets and farm animals were threatened by them.

12. We are planning a trip to Africa next year.

- The **tense** of a verb tells the time of the action or being. There are three simple tenses—present, past, and future.
- **Present tense** tells about what is happening now.
  - EXAMPLES: Conrad **is** busy. Conrad **studies** hard.
- **Past tense** tells about something that happened before.
  - EXAMPLE: Conrad **was** sick yesterday.
- **Future tense** tells about something that will happen. The auxiliary verbs <u>will</u> and <u>shall</u> are used in future tense.
  - EXAMPLES: Conrad **will take** the test tomorrow. I **shall keep** my word.

A. Complete each sentence by writing a verb in the tense shown in parentheses.

1. (future)   Hilary _____ tomorrow.

2. (future)   Kai _____ her up at the airport.

3. (past)   We _____ the house yesterday.

4. (past)   Carl _____ reservations for tomorrow night.

5. (present)   Hilary _____ my friend.

6. (future)   We _____ on a sightseeing tour.

7. (present)   I _____ very excited about Hilary's visit.

8. (past)   Margaret _____ Toby last week.

B. Write <u>present</u>, <u>past</u>, or <u>future</u> for the tense of each underlined verb.

1. Classes <u>will end</u> next month.   _____

2. We <u>studied</u> hard yesterday.   _____

3. Final exams <u>will start</u> soon.   _____

4. I <u>review</u> every evening.   _____

5. This method <u>worked</u> at midterm.   _____

6. I <u>got</u> A's on my tests then.   _____

7. Marty <u>studies</u> with me.   _____

8. We <u>will study</u> every evening this week.   _____

9. I hardly <u>studied</u> last year.   _____

10. My grades <u>showed</u> it, too.   _____

Present Perfect and Past Perfect Tenses

> - The **perfect tenses** express action that happened before another time or event.
> - The **present perfect** tense tells about something that happened at an indefinite time in the past. The present perfect tense consists of <u>has</u> or <u>have</u> + the past participle.
>   > EXAMPLES: I **have eaten** already. He **has eaten**, too.
> - The **past perfect** tense tells about something that happened before something else in the past. The past perfect tense consists of <u>had</u> + the past participle.
>   > EXAMPLE: I already **had eaten** when they arrived.

A. Write <u>present perfect</u> and <u>past perfect</u> for the tense of the underlined verbs.

_____ 1. Mei <u>had completed</u> high school in June.

_____ 2. She <u>had gone</u> to school in England before coming here.

_____ 3. Mei <u>has decided</u> that she likes her new school.

_____ 4. She <u>had been worried</u> that she wouldn't fit in.

_____ 5. Mei <u>has lived</u> in her house for eight months.

_____ 6. We <u>have tried</u> to make Mei feel welcome.

_____ 7. She <u>has told</u> us a great deal about England.

_____ 8. We <u>had known</u> England was an interesting place.

_____ 9. However, Mei <u>has described</u> things we never knew!

_____ 10. We <u>have decided</u> that we would like to visit Europe some day.

B. Complete each sentence with <u>have</u>, <u>has</u>, or <u>had</u> to form the verb tense indicated in parentheses.

1. (present perfect)   The pitcher _____ left the mound.

2. (present perfect)   The coach and catcher _____ talked to him.

3. (past perfect)   The coach _____ warned him to be careful.

4. (present perfect)   Jason _____ taken his place on the mound.

5. (past perfect)   Jason _____ pitched ten games by the end of last season.

6. (present perfect)   Jason _____ pitched very well.

7. (past perfect)   The team _____ won every game last week.

Using *Is/Are* and *Was/Were*

- Use <u>is</u> and <u>was</u> with a singular subject.   EXAMPLE: Here **is** Roberto.
- Use <u>are</u> and <u>were</u> with a plural subject.   EXAMPLE: There **are** Dr. Thomas and Dr. Williams.
- Always use <u>are</u> and <u>were</u> with the pronoun you.   EXAMPLES: You **are** my favourite cousin. You **are** late today.

- **Circle the verb that agrees with the subject of each sentence.**

1. Here (is, are) the box of paper clips you ordered.

2. There (is, are) three girls named Laura in our apartment building.

3. There (is, are) a small chance of showers tomorrow.

4. Mayor Laroche (is, are) going to speak today.

5. Here (is, are) the tools you asked me to bring.

6. There (is, are) much to be done.

7. Two of these chairs (is, are) damaged.

8. (Is, Are) these cars really being offered for sale?

9. Kelly, (is, are) this your car?

10. Many people (is, are) planning to go to the hockey game.

11. Xavier and I (was, were) afraid that Mario (was, were) not going to arrive on time.

12. Who (was, were) you talking to this afternoon?

13. A group of truck drivers (was, were) in the café.

14. There (was, were) many kinds of rare plants in the garden.

15. Several visitors (was, were) here this afternoon.

16. Anita, (wasn't, weren't) you interested in working overtime?

17. Why (wasn't, weren't) these dishes washed last night?

18. The mistakes in punctuation (was, were) carefully checked.

19. Raoul and Sara (wasn't, weren't) able to help us.

20. There (was, were) two large trays of sandwiches on the picnic table.

21. Each picture for the exhibit (was, were) carefully selected.

22. One of the sisters (was, were) enrolled at a university.

23. Each of the letters (was, were) read aloud.

24. (Was, Were) you planning to go to the park today?

25. Did you know that there (was, were) two new families in our apartment building?

26. (Wasn't, Weren't) you at the annual meeting, Ming?

27. Three of the people (was, were) injured when the accident occurred.

28. (Was, Were) your aunt and uncle the first to build a house on this block?

29. Who (was, were) the first settlers in your community?

Past Tenses of *Give, Take,* and *Write*

> ■ Never use a helping verb with <u>gave</u>, <u>took</u>, and <u>wrote</u>.
> ■ Always use a helping verb with <u>given</u>, <u>taken</u>, and <u>written</u>.

A. Underline the correct verb.

1. It (took, taken) the mechanic only a few minutes to change the tire.

2. Has anyone (took, taken) my note pad?

3. Who (wrote, written) the best letter?

4. I have (wrote, written) a thank-you note.

5. Tell me who (gave, given) you that address.

6. Have you (gave, given) the dog its food?

7. Bill hadn't (wrote, written) this poem.

8. Have you finally (wrote, written) for the tickets?

9. Emil had (gave, given) the lecture on boat safety yesterday at the YMCA.

10. Alicia and I (wrote, written) a letter to the editor.

11. Haven't you (took, taken) your seat yet?

12. We had our picture (took, taken) yesterday.

13. Who (gave, given) you these old magazines?

14. The workers (took, taken) all their equipment with them.

15. A friend had (gave, given) us the furniture.

16. Leslie had (wrote, written) the letter over three weeks ago.

17. Who (took, taken) the most photographs on the trip?

18. The doctor (gave, given) me a tetanus shot after I cut my hand.

19. Has Brian (wrote, written) to Julia yet?

B. Write the correct past tense form of each verb in parentheses to complete the sentences.

1. (take)   Amanda recently _____ her dog, Ralph, to the veterinarian.

2. (write) The doctor had _____ to say that Ralph needed his annual shots.

3. (give)   An assistant _____ Ralph a dog biscuit as soon as he arrived.

4. (give)   That way Ralph was _____ something that would distract him.

5. (take)   Before Ralph knew it, the doctor had _____ a sample of his blood.

6. (take)   It only _____ a minute to give Ralph his shots.

7. (give)   The doctor _____ Ralph a pat on the head.

8. (take)   "You have _____ very good care of Ralph," he said.

Past Tenses of *See, Go,* and *Begin*

> - Never use a helping verb with <u>saw</u>, <u>went</u>, and <u>began</u>.
> - Always use a helping verb with <u>seen</u>, <u>gone</u>, and <u>begun</u>.

A. Underline the correct verb.

1. The last person we (saw, seen) in the park was Eric.

2. Who has (went, gone) for the ice?

3. Marla and Yoko (began, begun) to fix the flat tire.

4. Charles (went, gone) to the supermarket for some lettuce.

5. Our summer vacation has (began, begun).

6. They had (saw, seen) a shooting star.

7. Hasn't she (went, gone) to the airport?

8. Yes, we (saw, seen) the concert poster.

9. Alice, have you ever (saw, seen) a penguin?

10. We never (went, gone) to hear the new mayor speak.

11. Olivia, why haven't you (began, begun) your work?

12. Mike (began, begun) to tell us about the accident.

13. Our guests have (went, gone).

14. It (began, begun) to snow early in the evening.

15. Work has finally (began, begun) on the new stadium.

16. We (saw, seen) our cousins last summer.

17. My three sisters (went, gone) to Toronto.

18. Have you (saw, seen) the waves pounding the huge boulders?

19. We (went, gone) to hear the symphony last night.

20. They (began, begun) their program with music by Mozart.

21. The program (began, begun) on time.

B. Write a sentence using each verb below.

1. saw _____

2. seen _____

3. gone _____

4. went _____

5. began _____

6. begun _____

Wear, Rise, Steal, Choose and Break

> - Never use a helping verb with <u>wore</u>, <u>rose</u>, <u>stole</u>, <u>chose</u>, and <u>broke</u>.
> - Always use a helping verb with <u>worn</u>, <u>risen</u>, <u>stolen</u>, <u>chosen</u>, and <u>broken</u>.

A. Underline the correct verb.

1. We almost froze because we hadn't (wore, worn) coats.

2. Haven't you (chose, chosen) a new shirt?

3. I (broke, broken) my new bike.

4. The river (rose, risen) more than a metre during the night.

5. Someone had (stole, stolen) our car last week.

6. Salina had (chose, chosen) many of our old landmarks for the city tour.

7. I have (wore, worn) these uncomfortable shoes for the last time.

8. We were far along the way when the sun (rose, risen).

9. The squirrels have (stole, stolen) most of our acorns.

10. The airplane (rose, risen) above the clouds.

11. The children have (wore, worn) a path through the backyard.

12. They (chose, chosen) to stay at the camp for a day.

13. Jan had (broke, broken) her leg the summer we visited her.

14. Have you ever (stole, stolen) home base?

15. Our pizza dough had (rose, risen) by the time we sliced the pepperoni.

16. The bottle's protective seal was (broke, broken), so we returned it to the store.

17. Kurt and Don (wore, worn) each other's clothes when they were younger.

18. The full moon had (rose, risen) over the deep, dark lake.

19. The jewel thief (stole, stolen) one too many diamonds before he got caught.

B. Circle any mistakes in the use of past tense verbs.

The sun had just rose when Kate recognized the familiar sound of fishing boats returning to shore. She hadn't meant to sleep late this morning, but the early morning waves had coaxed her back to sleep. Now, slipping into her sweatshirt, shoes, and damp shorts, Kate noticed that seagulls had again stole fish from the pail of bait. She chuckled at the thought, and then tossed the circling birds another minnow. Turning, Kate noticed Luke nearing the boat. He worn the same windbreaker and soft, leather shoes nearly every day since they first met, months ago. Kate paused for a moment. It occurred to her that she chosen a good friend. Luke had never broke a shoestring, or a promise.

- Never use a helping verb with <u>came</u>, <u>rang</u>, <u>drank</u>, <u>knew</u>, and <u>threw</u>.
- Always use a helping verb with <u>come</u>, <u>rung</u>, <u>drunk</u>, <u>known</u>, and <u>thrown</u>.

A. Underline the correct verb.

1. The tired horse (drank, drunk) from the cool stream.

2. The church bell has not (rang, rung) today.

3. I haven't (drank, drunk) my hot chocolate.

4. We (knew, known) that it was time to go.

5. Have you (threw, thrown) the garbage out?

6. Haven't the movers (came, come) for our furniture?

7. We (rang, rung) the fire alarm five minutes ago.

8. Haven't you (know, known) him for a long time?

9. I (threw, thrown) the ball to Gregor.

10. My friends from China (came, come) this afternoon.

11. Why haven't you (drank, drunk) your juice?

12. I always (came, come) to work in my wheelchair now.

13. I (knew, known) Pat when she was just a child.

14. Have you (threw, thrown) away last week's newspaper?

15. We have (came, come) to tell you something.

16. If you already (rang, rung) the bell, then you might try knocking.

17. Tony thinks he (drank, drunk) something that made him ill.

B. Write a sentence using each verb below.

1. came _____

2. come _____

3. rang _____

4. rung _____

5. threw _____

6. thrown _____

7. drank _____

8. drunk _____

9. knew _____

Eat, Fall, Draw, Drive, and Run

> - Never use a helping verb with <u>ate</u>, <u>fell</u>, <u>drew</u>, <u>drove</u>, and <u>ran</u>.
> - Always use a helping verb with <u>eaten</u>, <u>fallen</u>, <u>drawn</u>, <u>driven</u>, and <u>run</u>.

A. Underline the correct verb.

1. Taro, have you (drew, drawn) your diagram?

2. When we had (drove, driven) for two hours, we (began, begun) to feel hungry.

3. All of our pears have (fell, fallen) from the tree.

4. After we had (ate, eaten) our dinner, we (ran, run) around the lake.

5. A great architect (drew, drawn) the plans for our civic centre.

6. We had just (ran, run) into the house when we saw our friends.

7. Hadn't the building already (fell, fallen) when you (ran, run) around the corner?

8. Those heavy curtains in the theatre have (fell, fallen) down.

9. Last week we (drove, driven) to the lake for a vacation.

10. I have just (ate, eaten) a delicious slice of pizza.

11. I (ate, eaten) my breakfast before six o'clock this morning.

12. All of the leaves have (fell, fallen) from the elm trees.

13. When was the last time you (ran, run) a kilometre?

B. Write the correct past tense form of each verb in parentheses to complete the sentences.

1. (drive)   Last weekend we _____ to the lake for a picnic.

2. (draw)   Since Jenna knew several shortcuts, she _____ a detailed map for us.

3. (fall)   She mentioned that during a recent summer storm, debris _____ had

   on many of the roads.

4. (fall)   She warned us that a large tree _____ on one of the main roads.

5. (drive)   Jenna claimed that she had never _____ under such dangerous circumstances.

6. (run)   "I almost _____ right into that tree in the dark!" Jenna said.

7. (eat)   In order to avoid travelling at night, we _____ our dinner after
   we got home from the lake.

8. (eat)   We had _____ so much during our picnic that none of us minded waiting!

9. (draw)   Once home, we all agreed that Jenna had _____ a great map for us.

10. (run)   We made the trip in record time, and we hadn't _____ over any trees
    in the process!

Unit 3, Grammar and Usage

- Never use a helping verb with <u>did</u>.
  - EXAMPLE: Anne **did** a great job on her test.
- Always use a helping verb with <u>done</u>.
  - EXAMPLE: Hallie **had** also **done** a great job.
- <u>Doesn't</u> is the contraction of <u>does not</u>. Use it with singular nouns and the pronouns <u>he</u>, <u>she</u>, and <u>it</u>.
  - EXAMPLES: Rachel **doesn't** want to go. It **doesn't** seem right.
- <u>Don't</u> is the contraction of <u>do not</u>. Use it with plural nouns and with the pronouns <u>I</u>, <u>you</u>, <u>we</u>, and <u>they</u>.
  - EXAMPLES: Mr. and Mrs. Ricci **don't** live there. You **don't** have your purse.

A. Underline the correct verb.

1. Why (doesn't, don't) Lois have the car keys?

2. Show me the way you (did, done) it.

3. Have the three of you (did, done) most of the work?

4. Why (doesn't, don't) she cash a cheque today?

5. Please show me what damage the storm (did, done).

6. (Doesn't, Don't) the workers on the morning shift do a fine job?

7. Have the new owners of our building (did, done) anything about the plumbing?

8. (Doesn't, Don't) those apples look overly ripe?

9. Ira (doesn't, don't) want to do the spring cleaning this week.

10. The gloves and the hat (doesn't, don't) match.

11. Carolyn, have you (did, done) your homework today?

12. Who (did, done) this fine job of painting?

13. (Doesn't, Don't) the tile in our new kitchen look nice?

14. (Doesn't, Don't) that dog stay in a fenced yard?

15. He has (did, done) me a great favour.

16. I will help if he (doesn't, don't).

B. Write one sentence using <u>did</u> and one sentence using <u>done</u>.

1. _____

2. _____

C. Write one sentence using <u>doesn't</u> and one sentence using <u>don't</u>.

1. _____

2. _____

> - There are two kinds of action verbs: **transitive** and **intransitive**.
> - A transitive verb has a direct object.
>   > D.O.
>   > EXAMPLE: Jeffrey **painted** the house.
> - An intransitive verb does not need an object to complete its meaning.
>   > EXAMPLES: The sun **rises** in the east. She **walks** quickly.

A. Underline the verb in each sentence. Then write <u>T</u> for transitive or <u>I</u> for intransitive.

_____ 1. Kristina joined the health club in March.

_____ 2. She wanted the exercise to help her stay healthy.

_____ 3. Kristina exercised every day after work.

_____ 4. She became friends with Nancy.

_____ 5. They worked out together.

_____ 6. Nancy preferred the treadmill.

_____ 7. Kristina liked aerobics and running.

_____ 8. Sometimes they switched activities.

_____ 9. Nancy took an aerobics class.

_____ 10. Kristina used the treadmill.

_____ 11. Occasionally they swam in the pool.

_____ 12. Nancy was the better swimmer.

_____ 13. But Kristina had more fun.

_____ 14. She just splashed around in the water.

B. Underline the transitive verb, and circle the direct object in each sentence.

1. Kim walked Tiny every day.

2. Tiny usually pulled Kim along.

3. Kim washed Tiny every other week.

4. Tiny loved water.

5. He splashed Kim whenever he could.

6. Tiny also loved rawhide bones.

7. He chewed the bones until they were gone.

8. Kim found Tiny when Tiny was just a puppy.

- A **verbal** is a verb form that functions as a noun or adjective. There are three types of verbals: **infinitives**, **participles**, and **gerunds**.
- An **infinitive** is the base form of the verb, commonly preceded by <u>to</u>. An infinitive that functions as a noun is a verbal.
    - EXAMPLE: The object of the game is **to win**.
- A present or past **participle** that functions as an adjective is a verbal.
    - EXAMPLES: A **running** horse galloped down the road. **Dried** leaves flew from his hooves.
- A **gerund** is the present participle of a verb form ending in <u>-ing</u> that is used as a noun.
    - EXAMPLE: **Skiing** is her favourite sport.

A. Underline the infinitive in each sentence below.

1. Alan refused to quit.

2. The only thing he wanted was to finish.

3. Alan had trained to run this race for months.

4. It was not important to win.

5. Alan simply needed to finish.

6. He hoped to accomplish his goal.

7. Soon he was close enough to see the finish line.

B. Underline the participle in each sentence below.

1. Wayne and Shuster entertained the enlisted men in World War II.

2. The Windigo turned his blazing eyes on the frightened people.

3. The striking workers were chanting slogans.

4. Wilder Penfield was a leading brain surgeon.

5. The frozen pond made an ideal rink.

6. The flashing cards spelled a message.

7. The interested students studied hard.

C. Underline the gerund in each sentence below.

1. Studying is an important job.

2. Language arts and reading help improve your language ability.

3. Learning can be rewarding.

4. Memorizing is another skill you can learn.

5. Remembering is not always easy.

6. Do you think studying is time well spent?

7. Dancing is Lauren's favourite activity.

D. Underline the verbal in each sentence, and write <u>infinitive</u>, <u>participle</u>, or <u>gerund</u> on the line.

_____ 1. To act in a play is an honour.

_____ 2. Acting can be very exciting.

_____ 3. To write plays takes a lot of skill.

_____ 4. Working in the theatre is interesting.

_____ 5. Sally wanted to participate.

_____ 6. The hurried director got ready for the auditions.

_____ 7. Sally prepared a moving scene.

_____ 8. She was finally ready to read her scene.

_____ 9. Auditioning can scare anyone.

_____ 10. Sally's stirring performance won her a part.

_____ 11. Rehearsing can take up much time.

_____ 12. The actors must work long hours to memorize their parts.

_____ 13. Sally's convincing performance was outstanding.

_____ 14. All of the actors excelled in performing.

_____ 15. The smiling director congratulated the cast.

_____ 16. "To act is an art," said the director.

_____ 17. He called them all budding artists.

_____ 18. Performing is a pleasure for Yolanda.

_____ 19. Bowing is even more fun.

_____ 20. The audience could tell by Yolanda's face that she enjoyed

playing the part.

_____ 21. To continue her studies is her goal.

_____ 22. Acting is very important to Yolanda and Sally.

_____ 23. Interrupted lessons would distress them both.

_____ 24. They are consumed with acting.

_____ 25. They need constant practice to excel.

_____ 26. Well-rehearsed actors perform better.

   Unit 3, Grammar and Usage

Active and Passive Voice

> - **Voice** refers to the relation of a subject to its verb.
> - In the **active voice**, the subject acts.
>   EXAMPLE: **I painted** the house.
> - In the **passive voice**, the subject receives the action.
>   EXAMPLE: The house **was painted** by me.
> - Only transitive verbs are used in the passive voice.

A. Write A if the sentence is in the active voice and P if it is in the passive voice.

_____ **1.** Mahdi applied for a job in a grocery store.

_____ **2.** He needs money for gas and car repairs.

_____ **3.** He will handle the cash register.

_____ **4.** Mahdi will also stock the shelves.

_____ **5.** The application was turned in last week.

_____ **6.** The store's manager reads every application.

_____ **7.** Then the applicants are interviewed.

_____ **8.** Mahdi was interviewed on Monday.

_____ **9.** The manager was impressed by Mahdi.

_____ **10.** He will give Mahdi the job.

B. Rewrite each sentence in the active voice.

1. Caitlin was given a job babysitting by the McNeils.

_____

2. The children will be watched by her every day.

_____

3. Caitlin will be driven to their house by her friend.

_____

C. Rewrite each sentence in the passive voice.

1. Trina plays the drums in the band.

_____

2. She chose the drums because her father played drums.

_____

3. Trina won an award for her playing.

_____

- A **subject pronoun** is used in the subject of a sentence and after a linking verb.
  - EXAMPLES: **We** are going to the tournament. The woman in the suit is **she**.
- An **object pronoun** is used after an action verb or a preposition.
  - EXAMPLE: James threw the ball to **me**.
- A **possessive pronoun** is used to show ownership of something.
  - EXAMPLES. The red shoes are **mine**. Those are **my** red shoes.
- An **indefinite pronoun** does not refer to a specific person or thing.
  - EXAMPLE: **Someone** should take that history class.
- Use <u>who</u> as a subject pronoun, and use <u>whom</u> as an object pronoun.
  - EXAMPLES: **Who** is going to the party? We will ask **whom** to go with us?

A. Underline each correct pronoun.

1. Stephanie spoke to Jennifer and (I, me) about it.

2. Dean sent Tom and (they, them) some new shirts.

3. Please bring Anne and (I, me) some cool water.

4. Here comes (my, me) brother David.

5. Susan and (he, him) were late today.

6. Was it (she, her) who answered the knock?

7. I don't believe it was (they, them)!

8. Mona took Doug and (we, us) to work.

9. He told Steven and (she, her) about the problem.

10. Don't you think (someone, us) should help?

11. Raisa and (I, me) are going to work until seven o'clock.

12. It wasn't (your, yours) cat that meowed.

13. (He, Him) and Calvin are going to the game.

14. She told Denise and (my, me) about her fishing trip.

15. (Who, Whom) did you say got here early?

16. He said that it was (they, them) who came to our house.

17. (Everyone, We) will carry his or her own bundles.

18. It was (they, their) babysitter who knocked on the door.

19. (Who, Whom) did you meet for lunch?

20. Elizabeth and (she, her) always sit together.

21. This sweater is (hers, she).

22. (Who, Whom) led the band in the parade?

23. The red car is (our, ours).

24. Can you predict (who, whom) will win the election?

B. Underline each pronoun.

1. I told you to speak to him about our fishing trip.
2. Who is speaking?
3. They saw us when we passed by their house.
4. Just between you and me, I want to go with them.
5. He and Mike are going with us.
6. My decision to leave was made before our conversation.
7. Whom did you see?
8. This package was sent to you and me.
9. They are going with us to the game.
10. Jerry broke his arm.
11. Who told them?
12. She is my friend who moved to Mexico.
13. This cheque is mine.
14. Someone took some fresh flowers to them.
15. Who is she?
16. She went with us to the parade.
17. Barry, who is the president of that company?
18. Will she go with you?
19. Who telephoned me?
20. Should we eat with them at the picnic?
21. Which is your raincoat?
22. Did I tell you about our plans?
23. Which is mine?
24. Do you recall your sister's middle initial?
25. Why can't you come with us?
26. Did anybody get a letter?
27. You and I are on the list, too.
28. Did you see him?

C. Write sentences using the following pronouns:

1. theirs _____

2. you and I _____

3. you and me _____

4. them _____

5. anyone _____

> - An **antecedent** is the word to which a pronoun refers.
>   EXAMPLE: **Dogs** are dangerous if **they** bite.
> - A pronoun must agree with its antecedent in **gender** (**masculine**, **feminine**, or **neuter**) and in **number** (singular or plural).
>   EXAMPLES: **Sally** washed **her** hair. The **storm** changed **its** course. The **workers** went to **their** offices.
> - If the antecedent is an indefinite pronoun (one that doesn't refer to a specific person or thing), it is customary to use a masculine pronoun. However, it is now common to use both a masculine and a feminine pronoun.
>   EXAMPLES: **Someone** lost **his** gloves. **Someone** lost **his** or **her** gloves.

A. Underline each pronoun. Circle its antecedent.

1. Mike said he would tutor Carmen.

2. Carmen was doing poorly in her math class.

3. Carmen often shakes her head in confusion.

4. Mike promised to try his hardest.

5. Carmen worked on her math, but it was difficult.

6. Mike and Carmen said they would work every night.

7. The math test was coming, and it promised to be hard.

8. The class was ready for its test.

9. Carmen's palms were sweaty, and they felt clammy.

10. The teacher said he knew Carmen would do well.

11. When Carmen started the test, it didn't seem so hard.

12. Each student finished his or her test and put it on the instructor's desk.

13. The instructor would correct the tests and hand them back.

14. Carmen was pleased with her grade.

B. Circle the pronoun in parentheses that agrees with the antecedent.

1. Earl and Leon practised (their, his) free throws.

2. Each hoped practice would make (him, her) play better.

3. The team held (its, their) practice every day.

4. Leon practised (his, their) passing.

5. It is important to study the plays because (they, he) must be remembered.

6. Lee waxed (him, his) car.

7. The building was closed because (its, their) windows were damaged in the storm.

8. The flowers opened (its, their) petals in the sunshine.

9. Maggie found (his, her) book in the closet.

10. The guests piled (their, them) coats on the table.

Adjectives

- An **adjective** is a word that modifies a noun or a pronoun.
  - EXAMPLE: He likes **chocolate** cookies.
- Adjectives usually tell **what kind**, **which one**, or **how many**.
  - EXAMPLES: **bright** penny, **these** oranges, **twelve** classmates
- A **proper adjective** is an adjective that is formed from a proper noun. It always begins with a capital letter.
  - EXAMPLES: **Asian** continent, **English** language
- The articles <u>a</u>, <u>an</u>, and <u>the</u> are called **limiting adjectives**.

A. Write three adjectives to describe each noun.

1. mountains _____ _____ _____

2. weather _____ _____ _____

3. journey _____ _____ _____

4. classroom _____ _____ _____

5. book _____ _____ _____

B. Underline each adjective.

1. This old chair is comfortable.

2. We have read a funny story recently.

3. This heavy traffic creates many dangerous situations.

4. The eager sailors collected odd souvenirs at every port.

5. The tired, thirsty soldiers marched on.

6. This is my favourite book.

7. The solitary guard walked along the lonely beach.

8. We sat in the sixth row.

9. These damp matches will not strike.

10. Dan made French toast for breakfast.

11. Will you light those candles, please?

12. A red bird chirped loudly in the tall tree.

13. The heavy elephant sat down slowly.

14. A tour bus stopped at the pirate's cove.

15. The tall model wore Italian leather.

16. We ate fresh seafood on our vacation.

17. Do you like mashed or baked potatoes?

18. She served Chinese food for dinner.

Lesson
51
Demonstrative Adjectives

> - A **demonstrative adjective** is one that points out a specific person or thing.
> - <u>This</u> and <u>that</u> modify singular nouns. <u>This</u> points to a person or thing nearby, and <u>that</u> points to a person or thing farther away.
>   EXAMPLES: **This** movie is terrible. **That** sign is difficult to see.
> - <u>These</u> and <u>those</u> modify plural nouns. <u>These</u> points to persons or things nearby and <u>those</u> points to persons or things farther away.
>   EXAMPLES: **These** ribbons are the most colourful.
>   **Those** towels need to be folded.
> - The word <u>them</u> is a pronoun. Never use it to describe a noun.

- **Underline the correct demonstrative adjective.**

  1. Move (those, them) plants inside since it may freeze tonight.

  2. (These, That) box in front of me is too heavy to lift.

  3. Who brought us (those, them) delicious cookies?

  4. Look at (those, them) playful kittens.

  5. (That, Those) kind of friend is appreciated.

  6. (Those, Them) pictures are beautiful.

  7. What are (those, them) sounds I hear?

  8. Did you ever meet (those, them) people?

  9. We have just developed (these, them) photographs.

  10. Do you know any of (those, them) young people?

  11. May we take some of (these, them) folders?

  12. I have been looking over (these, them) magazines.

  13. Do not eat too many of (those, them) peaches.

  14. I do not like (this, these) kind of syrup.

  15. (Those, Them) people should be served next.

  16. Pasquale, please mail (these, them) letters.

  17. Look at (those, them) posters I made!

  18. (This, That) suburb is fifty kilometres away.

  19. (These, Them) antique coins are valuable.

  20. Look at (those, that) soccer players hustle!

  21. Zachary, may we see (these, them) photographs?

  22. Please return (that, these) library books.

  23. (These, Them) clothes need to be washed.

  24. Please hand me (that, those) plates.

  25. (Those, Them) cookies have nuts in them.

 Unit 3, Grammar and Usage

Comparing with Adjectives

- An adjective has three degrees of comparison: **positive**, **comparative**, and **superlative**.
- The simple form of the adjective is called the **positive** degree.
    EXAMPLE: Ian is **short**.
- When two people or things are being compared, the **comparative** degree is used.
    EXAMPLE: Ian is **shorter** than Oscar.
- When three or more people or things are being compared, the **superlative** degree is used.
    EXAMPLE: Ian is the **shortest** person in the group.
- For all adjectives of one syllable and a few adjectives of two syllables, add -er to form the comparative degree, and -est to form the superlative degree.
    EXAMPLE: smart—smarter—smartest
- For some adjectives of two syllables and all adjectives of three or more syllables, use more or less to form the comparative and most or least to form the superlative.
    EXAMPLES: This test is **more** difficult than I expected. Carol is the **most** generous of all. Kate is **less** talkative than Tom. Esther is the **least** talkative of all.

- **Complete each sentence with the correct degree of comparison of the adjective given in parentheses. Some of the forms are irregular.**

1. (changeable)   The weather seems _____ this year than last.

2. (faithful)   I think the dog is the _____ of all animals.

3. (agreeable)   Is James _____ than Sam?

4. (busy)   Theresa is the _____ person in the office.

5. (long)   Which is the _____ river, the Mississippi or the Amazon?

6. (lovely)   I think the rose is the of _____ all flowers.

7. (fresh)   Show me the _____ cookies in the store.

8. (high)   Which of the two mountains is _____ ?

9. (enjoyable)   Which is _____ , television or the movies?

10. (reckless)   That person is the _____ driver in town.

11. (young)   Of all the players, Olivia is the _____ .

12. (tall)   Alberto is the _____ of the three men.

13. (difficult)   Isn't the seventh problem _____ than the eighth?

14. (quiet)   We have found the _____ spot in the park.

Lesson 53 — Adverbs

> - An **adverb** is a word that modifies a verb, an adjective, or another adverb.
>   EXAMPLES: The rain poured **steadily**. His memories were **extremely** vivid.
>   She responded **very** quickly.
> - An adverb usually tells **how**, **when**, **where**, or **how often**.
> - Many adverbs end in -ly.

A. Underline each adverb.

1. The person read slowly but clearly and expressively.

2. Adam, you are driving too recklessly.

3. The airplane started moving slowly but quickly gained speed.

4. I spoke too harshly to my friends.

5. How did all of you get here?

6. I looked everywhere for my pen.

7. The man stopped suddenly and quickly turned around.

8. Stacy read that poem too rapidly.

9. Janice plays the guitar well.

10. The child was sleeping soundly.

11. The car was running noisily.

12. We returned early.

13. Those trees were severely damaged in the fire.

14. Frederick ran quickly, but steadily, in the race.

B. Write two adverbs that could be used to modify each verb.

1. read   _____   _____

2. think   _____   _____

3. walk   _____   _____

4. eat   _____   _____

5. sing   _____   _____

6. speak   _____   _____

7. dive   _____   _____

8. study   _____   _____

9. write   _____   _____

10. look   _____   _____

Lesson 54

Comparing with Adverbs

- An adverb has three degrees of comparison: **positive**, **comparative**, and **superlative**.
- The simple form of the adverb is called the **positive** degree.
    - EXAMPLE: Kathy ran **fast** in the race.
- When two actions are being compared, the **comparative** degree is used.
    - EXAMPLE: Amy ran **faster** than Kathy.
- When three or more actions are being compared, the **superlative** degree is used.
    - EXAMPLE: Maureen ran the **fastest** of all.
- Use -er to form the comparative degree and use -est to form the superlative degree of one-syllable adverbs.
- Use more or most with longer adverbs and with adverbs that end in -ly.
    - EXAMPLES: Louisa ran **more energetically** than Bob.
    - Ms. Baker ran the **most energetically** of all the runners.

A. Underline the adverb that best completes each sentence.

1. Mark arrived (sooner, soonest) than Greg.

2. Tony arrived the (sooner, soonest) of all.

3. They had to work very (hard, harder, hardest).

4. Tony painted (more, most) carefully than Mark.

5. Mark worked (faster, fastest) than Greg, so Mark painted the walls.

6. Lauren worked the (more, most) carefully of all.

B. Complete each sentence with the proper form of the adverb in parentheses.

1. (fast)   Jason wanted to be the _____ runner at our school.

2. (fast)   Costa could run _____ than Jason.

3. (seriously)   Jason trained _____ than he had before.

4. (frequently)   Jason is on the track _____ of all the runners.

5. (quickly)   Jason ran the sprint _____ than he did yesterday.

6. (promptly)   Jason arrives for practice _____ of anyone on the team.

7. (promptly)   He even arrives _____ than the coach!

8. (eagerly)   Costa does warm-up exercises _____ of all the runners.

9. (carefully)   Who concentrates _____ on his timing, Costa or Jason?

10. (hard)   The coach congratulates Jason on being the player who works the

_____ .

55

Prepositions

- A **preposition** is a word that shows the relationship of a noun or a pronoun to another word in the sentence.
  EXAMPLES: The child ran **into** the **house**. He put his boots **under** the **table**.
- These are some commonly used prepositions:

about	against	at	between	from	of	through	under
above	among	behind	by	in	on	to	upon
across	around	beside	for	into	over	toward	with

- **Underline each preposition in the sentences below.**

1. Can you draw a map <u>of</u> your area?

2. Who is the owner of this car?

3. The sugar maple is a common tree in Eastern Canada.

4. For whom are you waiting?

5. At the meeting, he spoke to me about your athletic ability.

6. Our company is proud of its industrious employees.

7. Her friend Cynthia stood beside her.

8. A small amount of that soup is all I want.

9. We went to the house at the end of the street.

10. Rowland Hill of England was the inventor of the adhesive postage stamp.

11. Most of the spectators stood during the last quarter of the game.

12. These shoes of mine are too tight at the heel.

13. We ate dinner at the new restaurant near the river.

14. They stood on the porch and watched for the mail carrier.

15. Anyone can succeed with hard work.

16. We walked behind that group.

17. Astronaut Roberta Bondar was the first Canadian woman in space.

18. A group of people on horses rode behind the band.

19. We walked to the picnic grounds during the lunch hour.

20. Ben slid down the slippery hill.

21. There is a bridge across the river in our town.

22. The ball was knocked over the fence and into the pond.

23. I see a spot of dirt under your left eye.

24. One can observe a strange world below the surface of an ocean.

25. The rocket quickly disappeared behind the clouds.

26. The captain of the team drank from the Stanley Cup.

27. Please sit between us.

28. This package is for you.

- A **phrase** is a group of closely related words used as a single part of speech but not containing a subject and predicate.
    - EXAMPLE: The writer **of this novel** is signing autographs.
- A **prepositional phrase** is a group of words that begins with a preposition and ends with a noun or pronoun.
    - EXAMPLE: He took the train **to Edmonton**.
- The noun or pronoun in the prepositional phrase is called the **object of the preposition**.
    - EXAMPLE: He took the train to **Edmonton**.

- **Put parentheses around each prepositional phrase. Then underline each preposition, and circle the object of the preposition.**

1. The airplane was flying (<u>above</u> the (clouds)).
2. We are moving to New Brunswick.
3. Sandra lives on the second block.
4. An old water tower once stood on that hill.
5. The car slid on the wet pavement.
6. Sealing wax was invented in the seventeenth century.
7. Motto rings were first used by the Romans.
8. Tungsten, a metal, was discovered in 1781.
9. Roses originally came from Asia.
10. The ball rolled into the street.
11. Do you always keep the puppies in a pen?
12. The children climbed over the fence.
13. She lives in Vernon, B.C.
14. Samuel de Champlain is called the father of New France.
15. They spread the lunch under the shade of the giant elm tree.
16. The treasure was found by a scuba diver.
17. A squad of soldiers marched behind the tank.
18. Shall I row across the stream?
19. Large airplanes fly across the country.
20. Walter looked into the sack.
21. The cat ran up the pole.
22. We visited the Alexander Graham Bell Museum in Nova Scotia.
23. Many tourists come to our region.
24. We spent last summer in the Fraser Valley.
25. Do not stand behind a parked car.

> - A prepositional phrase can be used to describe a noun or a pronoun.
>   Then the prepositional phrase is being used as an **adjective** to tell
>   which one, what kind, or how many.
>   EXAMPLE: The bird **in the tree** whistled.
>   The prepositional phrase <u>in the tree</u> tells **which** bird.
> - A prepositional phrase can be used to describe a verb. Then the prepositional
>   phrase is being used as an **adverb** to tell how, where, or when.
>   EXAMPLE: Charlie ate breakfast **before leaving for school**. The
>   prepositional phrase **before leaving for school** tells **when**
>   Charlie ate breakfast.

- **Underline each prepositional phrase, and classify it as adjective or adverb.**

1. They went <u>to the ranch</u>. *adv.*

2. The first savings bank was established in France.

3. Lake Winnipeg in Manitoba is my home.

4. Return all books to the public library.

5. Mark lives in an old house.

6. Tanya bought a sweater with red trim.

7. The birds in the zoo are magnificent.

8. Jade is found in Myanmar.

9. I spent the remainder of my money.

10. The magician waved a wand over the hat, and a rabbit appeared.

11. The diameter of a Sequoia tree trunk can reach three metres.

12. The capital of Poland is Warsaw.

13. The narrowest streets are near the docks.

14. Our family went to the movie.

15. Roald Amundsen discovered the South Pole in 1911.

16. The floor in this room is painted black.

17. The dead leaves are blowing across the yard.

18. A forest of petrified wood has been found.

19. The mole's tunnel runs across the lawn.

> - A **conjunction** is a word used to join words or groups of words.
>   EXAMPLES: Yuri **and** Brant have arrived. They worked **until** the sun went down.
> - These are some commonly used conjunctions:
> | | | | | | | |
> |---|---|---|---|---|---|---|
> | although | because | however | or | that | when | whereas |
> | and | but | if | since | though | whether | yet |
> | as | for | nor | than | unless | while | |
> - Some conjunctions are used in pairs. These include <u>either . . . or</u>, <u>neither . . . nor</u>, and <u>not only . . . but also</u>.

- **Underline each conjunction in the sentences below.**

1. Do you know whether Brandon is going to the employment office?

2. Jesse, are you and Ryan going to see a movie this afternoon?

3. Linda will go to the coast when the weather turns warm.

4. Gina or Vicki will take me to practice.

5. Are you and Elizabeth going swimming this Saturday?

6. Paul will be here unless he has to work.

7. Dean or I must go to the supermarket.

8. Tortière and potatoes are my favourite foods.

9. The trainer and the animals gave a good show.

10. I was angry at Megan because she was not on time.

11. Tom gets into trouble, but he usually gets out of it.

12. Carelessness is the cause of many falls and burns.

13. She stopped work because she had to leave early.

14. Matt has been understanding since I started working two jobs.

15. This chair is small, but it is comfortable.

16. Although it looked like rain, we went for a drive.

17. Kerry is two years older than Tom.

18. The remark was neither just nor kind.

19. You may go either by bus or by plane.

20. Tim is here, but he is too busy to help us right now.

21. Let's go inside, for it is getting dark.

22. We listened closely while the directions were given.

23. Fruit is not only delicious, but also healthful.

24. Bring either a short poem or a rhyme to class tomorrow.

25. Anne neither asked for help nor received any.

26. Neither Joe nor Marie went to the show.

A. Write the part of speech above each underlined word. Use the abbreviations given in the box.

1. A <u>heavy</u> dust <u>storm</u> <u>rolled</u> <u>across</u> the <u>prairie</u>.

2. This is <u>a</u> <u>nice</u> <u>surprise</u>!

3. The <u>dark</u> <u>clouds</u> <u>slowly</u> <u>gathered</u> in the north.

4. <u>Marlee</u> and <u>I</u> are showing slides <u>of</u> the photographs that <u>we</u> took on our <u>trip</u>.

5. Is the <u>capital</u> <u>of</u> <u>your</u> province built on a <u>river</u>?

6. <u>These</u> shrubs <u>are</u> <u>beautiful</u>.

7. <u>Someone</u> opened the door <u>very</u> <u>cautiously</u> <u>and</u> tiptoed inside.

8. Please <u>handle</u> <u>this</u> <u>extremely</u> fragile china <u>very</u> carefully.

9. <u>The</u> weary <u>people</u> waited <u>for</u> the <u>long</u> <u>parade</u> to start.

10. <u>Large</u> herds of <u>longhorn</u> cattle grazed on <u>these</u> <u>vast</u> plains.

11. <u>We</u> are going <u>to</u> the <u>new</u> <u>mall</u> <u>today</u>, <u>but</u> Sara can't go with us.

12. <u>Floyd</u>, <u>you</u> are eating <u>that</u> food <u>too</u> <u>rapidly</u>.

n.	noun
pron.	pronoun
v.	verb
adj.	adjective
adv.	adverb
prep.	preposition
conj.	conjunction

B. Write the plural form or the possessive form of the noun in parentheses.

1. (bench)   The park _____ need to be painted.

2. (fly)   The _____ landed on our picnic lunch.

3. (hero)   All of the _____ medals were awarded at the ceremony.

4. (pony)   Her _____ saddle has been cleaned and oiled.

5. (watch)   My _____ hands stopped moving.

C. Underline the appositive or appositive phrase, and circle the noun it identifies.

1. We plan to visit Washington, the capital of the United States, on our vacation.

2. My older sister Kira is an engineer.

3. We ate a hearty breakfast, pancakes and ham, before going to work.

D. Circle the correct verb.

1. A former resident (gave, given) this fountain to the city.

2. Was it the telephone or the doorbell that (rang, rung)?

3. Our guest speaker has (come, came) a little early.

4. Caroline has (know, known) Paul for ten years.

5. We asked Jan to (drive, driven) us to the movies.

6. Matt, haven't you (ate, eaten) the last piece of pineapple cake?

7. The frightened deer (ran, run) into the forest.

8. The Arnolds (gone, went) to Jamaica last January.

9. Andy (doesn't, don't) like to be late to work.

10. Chloe (took, taken) her brother to the zoo.

11. Susan (did, done) all of her chores before we went to the movie.

12. Jessica and I (is, are) ready to go, too.

13. Many of the trout (was, were) returned to the stream after the contest.

14. I have (began, begun) the study of Spanish.

15. A dead silence had (fell, fallen) upon the listeners.

16. Larry (wasn't, weren't) at work this morning.

E. Underline the verbal in each sentence, and write infinitive, participle, or gerund on the line.

_____ 1. The reason they went to the lake was to fish.

_____ 2. Skateboarding has become a popular sport.

_____ 3. The flashing lights warned people of danger.

_____ 4. Vladimir's goal is to finish law school.

_____ 5. The improved detergent cleaned better than the old formula.

F. Underline the pronoun in parentheses that agrees with the antecedent. Circle the antecedent.

1. Curtis and Erika tutored Hugh because (he, they) had missed the review.

2. The office workers had to leave (their, its) building when a fire started.

3. Bob and André brought the posters to (them, their) campaign office.

4. My sister collected baskets on (her, their) trip to Mexico.

5. The volunteers accepted donations and gave (it, them) to the charity.

A. Read the following paragraph.

Wilfrid (Wop) May was born in 1896 in Carberry, Manitoba. He is one of the most famous early Canadian bush pilots. May helped the RCMP to capture the elusive "Mad Trapper," who had shot a Mountie in the Yukon and then evaded capture for weeks in the middle of winter. It was the first time a plane had been used to catch a fugitive.

May flew many dangerous flights under even more difficult conditions. Once, a remote northern village reported an outbreak of smallpox. Unless a vaccine could be delivered to them right away, many people would die. Wop May volunteered to deliver the vaccine even though the only plane available had an open cockpit, and it was well below zero. May flew for hours to deliver that vaccine. Then, when he arrived, he had to turn around and head home right away, to avoid getting caught in a storm that was approaching. By the time he returned to Edmonton, he was frozen and exhausted, but he had saved those people's lives.

B. In the paragraph above, find four different pronouns and write them on the lines below.

1. _____ 2. _____ 3. _____ 4. _____

C. Find one proper adjective and the noun it describes.

1. _____

D. Find two demonstrative adjectives and the nouns they describe.

1. _____ 2. _____

E. Find two comparative adjectives.

1. _____ 2. _____

F. Find six prepositional phrases.

1. _____

2. _____

3. _____

4. _____

5. _____

6. _____

G. Find two conjunctions.

1. _____ 2. _____

                            Unit 3, Grammar and Usage

H. Rewrite the following paragraphs. Correct any mistakes in the use of possessive and plural nouns, pronouns, and verbs.

In the 1920s, many intrepid bush pilot open up the North. While the South already have a railway linking it from coast to coast, most of northern canadas community was as remote as ever. Pilot like Wop May and Punch Dickins helps to change all that by using remote lake and rivers as landing strip. In the 1920s them flew through largely uncharted areas, helping to spot forest fires, delivering mail, transporting peoples, and dropping off needed supply. On winter flight, the pilots have to drain the oil from his engines every night to stop it from freezing.

Today, small aircraft provides an invaluable service linking communities in the North. Many small communities has them own landing strips.

_____

_____

_____

_____

_____

_____

_____

_____

_____

_____

_____

_____

_____

_____

_____

_____

_____

_____

_____

_____

Using Capital Letters

- **Capitalize** the first word of a sentence and of each line of poetry.
    EXAMPLES: Mico recited a poem. The first two lines follow.
        All the animals looked up in wonder
        When they heard the roaring thunder.
- Capitalize the first word of a direct quotation.
    EXAMPLE: Beth said, "Let's try to memorize a poem, too."
- Capitalize the first, last, and all important words in the titles of books, poems, stories, and songs.
    EXAMPLES: *The Snow Walker*, "The Painted Door"

A. Circle each letter that should be capitalized. Write the capital letter above it.

1. Anthony said, "what time does the movie start?"

2. calixa lavallée wrote "o canada."

3. vanessa harwood is one of canada's best-known dancers.

4. paul asked, "when do you plan to visit your friend?"

5. who wrote the song "in the early morning rain"?

6. what famous canadian coined the phrase "he shoots, he scores"?

- Capitalize all **proper nouns**.
    EXAMPLES: Michael J. Fox, Mother, Portage Avenue, Italy, Alberta, Laurentian Mountains, Thanksgiving, November, Stanley Cup, *Bluenose*, British Columbia
- Capitalize all **proper adjectives**. A proper adjective is an adjective that is made from a proper noun.
    EXAMPLES: the Italian language, Chinese food, French tourists

B. Circle each letter that should be capitalized. Write the capital letter above it.

1. Lauren, does your friend live in vancouver, b.c., or carstairs, alberta?

2. The st. lawrence seaway links lake superior, lake huron, lake erie, and lake ontario.

3. The *pinta*, the *niña*, and the *santa maría* were the ships columbus sailed.

4. Some viking explorers may have landed in newfoundland before the french or the english arrived.

5. The founder of the canadian red cross was george ryerson.

6. Glaciers are found in the rocky mountains, the andes mountains, and the alps.

                    Unit 4, Capitalization and Punctuation

> - Capitalize a person's title when it comes before a name.
>   EXAMPLES: Mayor Flynn, Doctor Raman, Premier Kuhn
> - Capitalize abbreviations of titles.
>   EXAMPLES: Ms. C. Cooke, Dr. Pearsoll, Rev. Milne, Judge Brenner

C. Circle each letter that should be capitalized. Write the capital letter above it.

1. How long have you been seeing dr. thompson?

2. Our class invited mayor thomas to speak at graduation.

3. rev. tommy douglas of manitoba was the first leader of the New Democratic Party.

4. What time do you expect mr. and mrs. randall to arrive?

5. Most people believe premier johnston will win re-election.

6. At the ceremony, officer halden was honoured for his bravery.

7. When is ms. howell scheduled to begin teaching?

> - Capitalize abbreviations of days and months, parts of addresses, postal codes, and titles of members of the armed forces. Also capitalize all letters in the abbreviations of provinces.
>   EXAMPLES: Tues.; Nov.; 201 Main St. S.; Maj. Donna C. Plunkett; Guelph, ON; N1H 2B3

D. Circle each letter that should be capitalized. Write the capital letter above it.

1. niles school art fair

   sat., feb. 8th, 9 a.m.

   110 elm dr. n.

2. rockwood

   june 23–24

   rockwood lake

   rockwood, on n1g 4l3

3. october fest

   october 28 and 29

   9 a.m.–5 p.m.

   63 maple st.

4. barbara dumont

   150 telson rd.

   vegreville, alberta t9c 1t9

5. captain c. j. neil

   c/o *ocean star*

   p.o. box 4455

   vancouver, bc v6b 1x7

6. dr. rupert b. stevens

   elmwood memorial hospital

   1411 first street

   st. john's nf a1e 6b4

E. Write a sentence to show each use of capital letters.

1. Name of a holiday _____

_____

2. Name of a restaurant in your community _____

_____

3. Name of a favourite book _____

_____

4. Name of an author _____

_____

5. Name of a business firm in or near your community _____

_____

6. Name of a country _____

_____

7. Name of a song _____

_____

8. Name of a magazine _____

_____

9. A direct quotation _____

_____

10. Name of a musician _____

_____

11. A title that is written as part of a name _____

_____

12. Name of a university or college _____

_____

13. Name of a river or lake _____

_____

14. Name of an actor or actress _____

_____

Using End Punctuation

> - Use a **period** at the end of a declarative sentence.
>   EXAMPLE: Sunlight is essential for the growth of plants.
> - Use a **question mark** at the end of an interrogative sentence.
>   EXAMPLE: How much sunlight does a plant need?

A. Use a period or question mark to end each sentence below.

1. Doesn't Sandra's family now live in Montréal ____

2. "David," by Earle Birney, is a well-known poem ____

3. Isn't someone knocking at the door, Beth ____

4. Didn't Janice ask us to meet her at 2:30 this afternoon ____

5. In Calgary, we visited the Glenbow Museum ____

6. The greatest library in ancient times was in Alexandria, Egypt ____

7. Aren't the employees' cheques deposited in a different bank ____

8. Will Ms. Wilson start interviewing applicants at 10:00 a.m. ____

9. My uncle has moved to Calgary, Alberta ____

10. Corn, oats, and soybeans are grown in Iowa ____

11. Isn't Alex the chairperson of our committee ____

12. I've mowed the lawn, pulled the weeds, and raked the leaves ____

13. Did the Battle of Batoche end the North West Rebellion ____

14. Is El Salvador in Central America ____

B. Add the correct end punctuation where needed in the paragraphs below.

Did you know that experts say dogs have been around for thousands of years ____ In fact, they were the first animals to be made domestic ____ The ancestors of dogs were hunters ____ Wolves are related to domestic dogs ____ Like wolves, dogs are social animals and prefer to travel in groups ____ This is called pack behaviour ____

There have been many famous dogs throughout history ____ Can you name any of them ____ In the eleventh century, one dog, Saur, was named king of Norway ____ The actual king was angry because his people had removed him from the throne, so he decided to make them subjects of the dog ____ The first dog in space was a Russian dog named Laika ____ Laika was aboard for the 1957 journey of *Sputnik* ____ Most people have heard of Rin Tin Tin and Lassie ____ These dogs became famous in movies and television ____

There are several hundred breeds of dogs throughout the world ____ The smallest is the Chihuahua ____ A Chihuahua weighs less than one kilogram ____ Can you think of the largest ____ A Saint Bernard or a Mastiff can weigh over 70 kilograms ____

- Use a **period** at the end of an imperative sentence.

    EXAMPLE: Open this jar of tomatoes for me, please.

- Use an **exclamation point** at the end of an exclamatory sentence and after an interjection that shows strong feelings. If a command expresses great excitement, use an exclamation point at the end of the sentence.

    EXAMPLES: Look at the stars! Ouch! I'm so excited!

C. Add periods or exclamation points where needed in these sentences below.

1. Answer the telephone, Michael ___

2. Please clean the kitchen for me ___

3. Oh I can't believe how late it is ___

4. Hurry The plane is leaving in a few minutes ___

5. Carry the bags to the check-in counter ___

6. Then run to the waiting area ___

7. Hold that seat for me ___

8. I can't miss the flight ___

9. Stop ___ Stop ___ You forgot your ticket ___

10. Please slow down ___

11. Sit down, and put on your seat belt ___

12. We're off ___

13. Look how small the city is ___

14. Please put on your seat belt ___

15. Obey the captain's orders ___

16. I can't wait until we land ___

17. Please give me that magazine ___

18. Look ___ We're about to land ___

D. Add the correct end punctuation where needed in the paragraphs below.

Mr. Henry Modine lives in Vancouver, B.C. ___ He often exclaims, "What a wonderful town ___" What do you think he does for a living ___ Mr. Modine owns a fishing boat, *The Chinook* ___ In all of Vancouver, there are few boats as fine as *The Chinook* ___ Henry Modine named his boat after the fish his customers like the best – chinook salmon ___ Henry guarantees his customers a fish if they come out on his boat ___

"Fantastic ___" shouts Henry when someone hooks a salmon ___ Henry then says "Bring it in ___" Part of Henry's job is to help the fishers reel in the fish ___ Did you know that some salmon grow as long as one metre ___ Most of the ones Henry's customers catch measure about 50 centimetres ___ They are delicious if they are cooked right away ___

Unit 4, Capitalization and Punctuation

Using Commas

- Use a **comma** between words or groups of words that are in a series.
  - EXAMPLE: Peaches, plums, and cherries belong to the rose family.
- Use a comma before a conjunction in a compound sentence.
  - EXAMPLE: The farmers planted many crops, and they will work long hours to harvest them.
- Use a comma after a subordinate clause when it begins a sentence.
  - EXAMPLE: After we ate dinner, we went to a movie.

A. Add commas where needed in the sentences below.

1. Frank Magda and Patricia are planning a surprise party for their parents.

2. It is their parents' fiftieth wedding anniversary and the children want it to be special.

3. They have invited the people their parents used to work with their golf club members and long-time friends of the family.

4. Even though the children are grown and living in their own homes it will be hard to make it a surprise.

5. Mr. and Mrs. Slaughter are active friendly and involved in many things.

6. For the surprise to work everyone will have to be sure not to say anything about their plans for that day.

7. This will be especially hard for the Knudsens but they will do their best.

8. Since every Sunday the families have dinner together the Knudsens will have to become very good actors the week of the party.

- Use a comma to set off a quotation from the rest of a sentence.
  - EXAMPLES: "I want to go with you," said Paul.
    Paul said, "I want to go with you."

B. Add commas before or after the quotations below.

1. "We're sorry that we have to cancel our plans" said Earl.

2. Pina said "But we've done this every week for ten years!"

3. Jeanette said "We have to leave town."

4. Ivan asked "Can't you put it off just one day?"

5. "No I'm afraid we can't" said Earl.

6. "Then we'll just start over the following week" said Pina cheerfully.

7. Jeanette said "I bet no one else has done this."

8. "I sure hate to spoil our record" said Earl.

9. "Don't worry about it" said Ivan.

10. "Yes everything will work out" said Jeanette.

- Use a comma to set off the name of a person who is being addressed.
  - EXAMPLE: Emily, are you ready to go?
- Use a comma to set off words like yes, no, well, and oh at the beginning of a sentence.
  - EXAMPLE: Yes, as soon as I find my jacket.
- Use a comma to set off an appositive.
  - EXAMPLE: Felix, Emily's dog, is entered in a dog show.

C. Add commas where needed in the sentences below.

1. Anthony a grocery store owner was planning for a busy day.
2. "Diane would you open the store at 9 o'clock?" said Anthony.
3. "Of course that's the time we always open," said Diane.
4. "Pierre the chef at Elaine's will be coming by," he said.
5. Kelly said "Stephanie I'd like some fresh peanuts."
6. "Yes but how many pounds would you like?" answered Stephanie.
7. Ms. Harmon asked "Martin what kind of fresh fruit do you have?"
8. "Well let me check what came in this afternoon," said Martin.
9. Alan the butcher had to wait on fifteen customers.
10. "I don't have time to wait Alan," said Carol.
11. The manager Jamal told everyone to be patient.
12. "Please it will go quickly if you all take a number," said Jamal.
13. "Yes you're right as usual," said the crowd.
14. Martin the produce manager went behind the counter to help.
15. Well they had sold all of their grapes and tomatoes before noon.
16. "We only have one bushel of green beans left" said Martin.
17. Mr. Loster bought cherries bananas and corn.
18. He was planning a special dinner for Sara his wife.
19. Mr. Loster spent the afternoon cooking baking and cleaning.
20. Today July 18 was her birthday.

D. Add commas where needed in the paragraph below.

Men women boys and girls from across Canada participate in the Special Olympics. Because of this event patterned after the Olympic games boys and girls with disabilities have opportunities to compete in a variety of sports. The Special Olympics includes competition in track swimming and gymnastics. Volunteers plan carefully and they work hard to insure that the event will be challenging rewarding and worthwhile for all the participants. One of my neighbours Chris Bell once worked as a volunteer. "It was an experience that I'll never forget" he said.

Lesson
62
Using Quotation Marks and Apostrophes

> - Use **quotation marks** to show the exact words of a speaker. Use a comma or another punctuation mark to separate the quotation from the rest of the sentence. A quotation may be placed at the beginning or at the end of a sentence. Begin the quotation with a capital letter.
>   - EXAMPLES: Pat said, "Please take the dog for a walk." "Please take the dog for a walk," said Pat.
> - A quotation may also be divided within the sentence.
>   - EXAMPLE: "Pat," said Scott, "I just returned from a walk!"

A. Add quotation marks and commas where needed in the sentences below.

1. Wait for me said Laura because I want to go with you.

2. Kim, did you write an article about spacecraft? asked Tom.

3. Where is the manager's desk? inquired the stranger.

4. Joanne asked What is Eric's address?

5. Harry asked How long did Queen Victoria rule the British Empire?

6. Eugene, did you bring your interesting article? asked the teacher.

7. Good morning said Cindy.

8. Doug asked Did Jim hurt himself when he fell?

9. The meeting begins in ten minutes said Rico.

10. Hoan, you're early said Melissa.

11. Come on, said the coach you'll have to play harder to win this game!

12. Tony said, I know you'll do well in your new job. You're a hard worker.

> - Use an **apostrophe** in a contraction to show where a letter or letters have been taken out.
>   - EXAMPLES: I **can't** remember your name. **I'll** have to think about it.
> - Use an apostrophe to form a possessive noun. Add -'s to most singular nouns. Add -' to most plural nouns. Add -'s to a few nouns that have irregular plurals.
>   - EXAMPLES: **Dina's** house is made of brick. All the **neighbours'** houses are wooden. The **children's** treehouse is wooden.

B. Write the words in which an apostrophe has been left out. Insert apostrophes where they are needed.

1. Kate, didnt you want Sues job? _____

2. Havent you seen Pauls apartment? _____

3. Stuart didnt hurt himself when he fell off Toms ladder. _____

4. The employees paycheques didnt arrive on time. _____

- Use a **colon** after the greeting in a business letter.
  EXAMPLES: Dear Mr. Johnson: Dear Sirs:
- Use a colon between the hour and the minute when writing the time.
  EXAMPLES: 1:30   6:15   11:47
- Use a colon to introduce a list.
  EXAMPLE: Our grocery list included the following items: chicken, milk, eggs, and broccoli.

A. Add colons where needed in the sentences below.

1. At 2 1 0 this afternoon, the meeting will start.

2. Please bring the following materials with you pencils, paper, erasers, and a notebook.

3. The meeting should be over by 4 3 0.

4. Those of you on the special committee should bring the following items cups, paper plates, forks, spoons, and napkins.

5. The meeting will deal with the following pool hours, swimming rules, and practice schedules.

6. The lifeguards will meet this evening from 8 0 0 to 1 0 0 0 to discuss responsibilities.

7. We will read the letter at 3 0 0 and have a question-and-answer session.

- Use a **hyphen** between the parts of some compound words.
  EXAMPLES: twenty-one   sister-in-law   go-getter   well-behaved
  air-conditioned   middle-aged   sixty-six   great-grandfather
  blue-green   old-fashioned   second-storey   ninety-two
- Use a hyphen to separate the syllables of a word that is carried over from one line to the next.
  EXAMPLE: When the coach has finished his speech, the class members will be allowed to use the pool.

B. Add hyphens where needed in the sentences below.

1. We decided to attend a class on how to use less water when garden ing.

2. Our lawn and old fashioned flower gardens need too much water.

3. The sign up sheet at the door was for those who wanted to be on a mailing list.

4. Twenty seven people had already signed up.

5. We saw that our son and daughter in law were there, too.

6. Hank spotted them sitting on an aisle near the centre of the audi torium.

7. The speaker was a well known expert on gardening.

8. We sat next to our family and learned about long term plans for water conservation.

A. Circle each letter that should be capitalized. Then add the correct end punctuation.

1. mr. j. c. moran owns a car dealership in edison, alberta ___

2. jesse decided to apply for a job on tuesday ___

3. wow, mr. moran actually offered him a job ___

4. jesse will start work in june ___

5. jesse is the newest employee of moran's cars and vans ___

6. didn't he get auto experience when he lived in ontario ___

7. he also got training at dunwoody technical institute ___

8. jesse took some computer courses there taught by mr. ted woods and ms. jane hart ___

9. jesse had temporary jobs at highland cafe and mayfield electronics for the last two years ___

10. since jesse wants to be prepared for his new job, he checked out *automobile technology and the automobile industry* from the wyndham library ___

B. Add commas where needed in the sentences below.

1. After Jesse got the new job his family friends and neighbours gave him a party.

2. Everyone brought food drinks and even some gifts.

3. Bob Jesse's roommate and Charlotte Jesse's sister bought him a briefcase.

4. His mother and father bought him a new shirt jacket and tie for his first day on the job.

5. His father congratulated him by saying "Jesse we are happy for you and we wish you the best in your new job."

6. Jesse replied "Well I'm also very excited about it and I want to thank all of you for the party and the gifts."

C. Add commas and quotation marks where needed in the sentences below.

1. How did you get so lucky Jesse? asked Mike.

2. It wasn't luck answered Jesse because I studied before I applied for this job.

3. I didn't know you could study to apply for a job said Mike laughing.

4. Mike I read an employment guide before I applied said Jesse.

5. I have never heard of an employment guide! exclaimed Mike.

6. It's a great book said Jesse.

7. Jesse I'd like to apply for a job at Moran's said Mike.

8. Jesse replied Why don't you read my guide to prepare for the interview?

D. Insert apostrophes, colons, and hyphens where needed in the sentences below.

1. Joe King, Jesses best friend, is the one who gave Jesse the employment guide to use for his interview at Morans.

2. Jesse didnt know important interview skills.

3. The guide offered twenty five helpful hints.

4. The guide suggested the following dress neatly, be on time, be polite, and be enthusiastic.

5. Jesse also used the guides suggestions for preparing a résumé listing his work experience.

6. Jesses list contained these items his employers names and addresses, dates of employment, and job descriptions.

7. The guide said Jesse should be a well informed applicant, so he researched salespersons duties and made a list of questions to ask.

8. Jesses guide recommended getting to the interview early to have time to fill out the employers application forms.

9. Jesse arrived at Mr. Morans office at 345 for his 400 interview.

10. The interview lasted forty five minutes, and Jesse was relaxed and self confident when he left.

11. Mr. Morans phone call the next day at 130 let Jesse know he had gotten the job.

12. Jesse needed to do the following pick up a salespersons manual, fill out employment forms, and enroll in the companys insurance program.

E. Punctuate the letter below. Circle each letter that should be capitalized.

73 river st. e

edson, ab t7e 1a7

may 30, 1997

Dear mr. moran,

I just wanted to thank you for offering me the salespersons position with your company __ you mentioned in our interview that my duties would be the following selling cars and vans checking customers credit references and assisting customers with their paperwork __ ive studied the automobile sales guide that you gave me and i feel that im prepared to do a terrific job for morans __ thank you again im looking forward to starting next monday __

sincerely,

jesse pavlicek

 Unit 4, Capitalization and Punctuation

A. Circle each letter that should be capitalized below. Add punctuation where needed.

720 w. raven

swift current, sk s9h 3b4

may 4, 1997

Dear sirs:

on may 3, 1997, i received the compact disc player i had ordered from your catalogue ___ the following pieces were missing from the package the battery pack the high quality headphones and the adapter ___ please let me know what i should do about this ___ will you send the pieces or should I return the whole package ___ since your motto is that customers happiness is your goal i thought i would let you know that im not very happy about this ___ ive ordered other things in the past ___ they were great ___ what happened to my order this time ___ im waiting anxiously for your answer ___

Sincerely yours,

bonnie williams

B. Circle each letter that should be capitalized. Add punctuation where needed.

478 beacon st.

london, on n5y 6b8

june 1, 1997

Dear ms. williams:

please excuse us ___ this is awful ___ do send the entire package back and we will replace it ___ how can we apologize properly ___ first, we will send your new compact disc player special delivery so you will get it quickly ___ second, we will enclose a copy of *sounds of the nineties* for your pleasure ___ we are sorry ___ thank you for your past orders ___ our customers happiness is our major goal ___ well do everything we can to make sure that this order goes through properly ___ please let us know if everythings there ___ we look forward to hearing from you ___

Gratefully yours,

the sound team

C. Rewrite the letter below. Capitalize any letters that should be capitalized. Add needed punctuation.

720 w. raven

swift current, sk s9h 3b4

june 27, 1997

Dear sound team:

hurray ___ my compact disc player arrived today and its great ___ thank you ___ now when I walk my dog i can listen to a CD ___ thank you also for *sounds of the nineties* ___ can you believe it ___ i have a copy of *tunes of the eighties* and had planned to buy *sounds of the nineties* ___ now i dont have to ___ thats great ___

I also want to thank you for your courteous letter ___ im sure mistakes can happen to anyone ___ everyones quick action was greatly appreciated ___ your letter and package arrived at 10 00 this morning ___ youre fantastic ___

Sincerely,

bonnie williams

_____

_____

_____

_____

_____

_____

_____

_____

_____

_____

_____

_____

_____

_____

_____

 Unit 4, Capitalization and Punctuation

Lesson
64

Writing Sentences

- Every sentence has a base consisting of a simple subject and a simple predicate.

  EXAMPLE: <u>Amanda</u> <u>baked</u>.

- Expand the meaning of a sentence by adding adjectives, adverbs, and prepositional phrases to the sentence base.

  EXAMPLE: **My cousin** Amanda baked **a delicious orange cake for dessert**.

A. Expand the meaning of each sentence base by adding adjectives, adverbs, and/or prepositional phrases. Write each expanded sentence below.

1. (Carson swam.)

_____

2. (Clock ticked.)

_____

3. (Snow falls.)

_____

4. (Sun rose.)

_____

5. (Fireworks exploded.)

_____

B. Imagine two different scenes for each sentence base below. Write an expanded sentence to describe each scene you imagine.

1. (Students listened.) **a.** _____

  b. _____

2. (Ewan wrote.) **a.** _____

  b. _____

3. (Kamal played.) **a.** _____

  b. _____

4. (Axel drove.) **a.** _____

  b. _____

5. (We helped.) **a.** _____

  b. _____

Unit 5, Composition

© 1997 Gage Educational Publishing Company

91

Writing Topic Sentences

> ■ A topic sentence states the main idea of a paragraph. It is often placed
> at the beginning of a paragraph.
>
> EXAMPLE:
> **Ray was asked to write an article about the new recreation
> centre for the school paper.** He wrote a list of questions to ask. He
> interviewed the park superintendent. He found out about the old park
> and why it was necessary to build a recreation centre.

A. Underline the topic sentence in each paragraph below.

1.   Ray knew that having good questions was very important to a successful interview.

He thought carefully about what he wanted to know. Then he divided his questions into groups.

Some were about the building. Some were about recreation. Others were about the staff.

2.   He wanted to include something about the history of the park. He found out who first owned

the land. He also asked how people had used the park over the years.

3.   Ray found out that the park was nearly as old as the town itself. It had been the scene

of picnics, baseball games, carnivals, concerts, and holiday festivals. Political meetings had

also been held there.

B. Write a topic sentence for each group of sentences below.

1. **Topic Sentence:** _____

   a. James Leland was the park superintendent.
   b. He had worked in the field of recreation and sports all his adult life.
   c. His father had been a high school teacher and coach.
   d. His grandfather had been a popular baseball player.

2. **Topic Sentence:** _____

   a. Ray enjoyed talking to James.
   b. He found out more than he had ever expected.
   c. James told him why the community needed the centre.
   d. The city had grown, and it needed to provide recreation for its residents.

**C. Think of a topic you are interested in. Write the topic on the line. Then write a
topic sentence.**

Topic: _____

Topic Sentence: _____

_____

> ■ The idea expressed in the topic sentence can be developed with sentences containing **supporting details**. Details can include facts, examples, and reasons.

A. Circle the topic sentence, and underline only the sentences containing supporting details in the paragraph below.

Ray asked Theresa to help him with the article. She would write out the tape-recorded interviews. She would also make suggestions for changes. Theresa is very athletic. Finally, they would both work on typing the article.

B. After each topic sentence, write five sentences containing supporting details.

1. You must be organized when writing an article.

    a. _____

    b. _____

    c. _____

    d. _____

    e. _____

2. It is important to learn all you can about your topic.

    a. _____

    b. _____

    c. _____

    d. _____

    e. _____

C. Write four sentences that contain supporting details for the topic sentence you wrote in Exercise C, page 92.

Topic Sentence: _____

    a. _____

    b. _____

    c. _____

    d. _____

> - One way to organize information in a paragraph is to put it in **chronological order**—the time in which events occurred. Words such as first, next, second, then, finally, and later are used to indicate the order in which events happen.   EXAMPLE: **First**, Ray checked his tape recorder. **Then** he left for the interview.
> - Another way to organize information is to use **spatial order**. Words such as above, near, over, beside, right, left, closer, farther, up, and down are used to express spatial relationships.   EXAMPLE: The eagle sat on **top** of the tree. He watched the pond **below**.

A. Read each paragraph below and tell whether it is in chronological order or spatial order. For the paragraph in chronological order, underline the time order words. For the paragraph in spatial order, underline the words that indicate spatial order.

1.   The park board of directors must first approve the architect's design for the recreation centre. Then they must develop and approve a budget for the construction of the centre. Finally, they can give approval to construction of the centre.

   Order: _____

2.   The plan for the recreation centre includes play areas for young children. A slide and swingset will be built next to a large sand box. A jungle gym will be to the left of the slide. Children will be able to climb to the top of the jungle gym and then jump down to the ground.

   Order: _____

B. Number the details below in chronological order.

   _____ Then, early in March, the park board of directors approved the architect's design.

   _____ Next, the budget was approved in April.

   _____ The centre's roof was finally completed in August.

   _____ In January, the architect first finished his design.

C. Choose one of the scenes below. Write a paragraph of at least four sentences describing the scene. Use spatial order words to show location.

   Scenes: your house, a ballpark, a restaurant, a theatre, a friend's house

   _____

   _____

   _____

   _____

Topic and Audience

- The **topic** of a story or an article is the subject written about.
- The **audience** is the group of readers.
  EXAMPLES: students, family members, neighbours, readers of a newspaper

A. Choose the most likely audience for each topic listed below.

     a. first-graders   **b.** the city council   **c.** high-school students   **d.** parents

_____ **1.** Star Athlete Visits Students at Recreation Centre

_____ **2.** Study Shows Connection between Time Spent Exercising and Student Progress in School

_____ **3.** Peter Rabbit Here for Hop and Jump Exercises

_____ **4.** Council Considers Tax Plans to Finance Recreation Centre

_____ **5.** Tryouts for High School Track Team on Friday

_____ **6.** Study Shows City Budget Shortfall Next Year

_____ **7.** Kelsey School Parents' Night Next Thursday

_____ **8.** Officer Safety to Visit Young Students Next Week

_____ **9.** University Considers Raising Tuition

_____**10.** Council Approves Funds to Expand City Bus Service

B. Read the paragraph below. Then answer the questions that follow.

On Tuesday evening, May 2, 1997, at 6:00, Hawkeye, the mascot of the Child Protection Foundation, will be at the park with his handler, Officer Roy Meyers. While Hawkeye, the long-eared hound, entertains the youngsters, Officer Meyers will discuss the topic "Keeping Your Children Safe." This unusual pair has travelled across the country to introduce the findings on topics such as accidents in the home, hazardous toys, and bike safety.

1. What is the topic of the paragraph?

_____

2. Name two possible audiences for the paragraph.

_____

3. Explain why each audience might be interested.

    Audience 1: _____

    Audience 2: _____

C. Choose a topic in which you are interested. Write the name of the topic, and name the audience it would be most likely to interest.

    Topic: _____

    Audience. _____

- A **clustering diagram** shows how ideas relate to a particular topic. The topic is written in the centre. Related ideas are written around the topic. Lines show the connections between the ideas.

EXAMPLE:

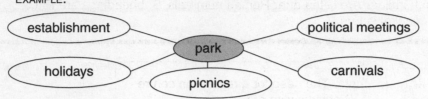

establishment   political meetings

park

holidays   carnivals

picnics

Topic Sentence: The recreation centre will be built on land that was once a park.

A. Read each paragraph below. Notice the underlined topic sentence as you read. Then fill in each cluster to show how the details relating to that topic sentence could have been chosen.

1. <u>Ray had a great deal of work to do for the article.</u> He had to finish the interviews, decide what information to use, and write a rough draft. He then had to revise the draft, type the final copy, and proofread it.

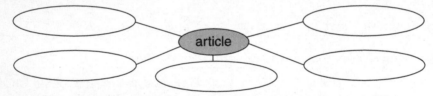

article

2. <u>Theresa worked hard on the article.</u> She typed the interviews. She edited the article. She organized the rough draft. Finally, she helped with the final revision and proofreading.

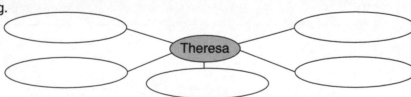

Theresa

B. Rewrite the topic sentence you wrote on page 93, Exercise C.

Topic Sentence: _____

C. Write that topic from Exercise B in the centre of the cluster below. Then fill in the cluster with details that would support your main topic.

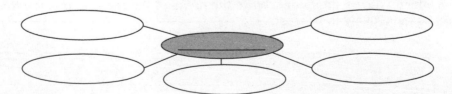

- Before you write about a topic, organize your thoughts by making an **outline**. An outline consists of the title of the topic, **main headings** for the main ideas, and **subheadings** for supporting ideas.
- Main headings are listed after Roman numerals. Subheadings are listed after capital letters.

Topic: The need for a recreation centre
  I. Problems with park
    A. Age of equipment
    B. Limited usefulness for residents
  II. Advantages of recreation centre
    A. Wide range of uses
    B. Safe, up-to-date equipment

- **Refer to your topic sentence on page 96, Exercise B. Write an outline based on the clusters, using the example outline as a guide.**

Topic: _____

I. _____

   A. _____

   B. _____

II. _____

   A. _____

   B. _____

III. _____

   A. _____

   B. _____

IV. _____

   A. _____

   B. _____

V. _____

   A. _____

   B. _____

Lesson 71

Preparing Interview Questions

- Writers use interviews to get information. Good interview questions will encourage the person being interviewed to talk freely about the subject.
    EXAMPLES: Why do we need a recreation centre? Who will be involved in making decisions?
- Avoid questions that can be answered either <u>yes</u> or <u>no</u> by beginning them with words such as <u>who</u>, <u>what</u>, <u>why</u>, and <u>how</u>.
    EXAMPLE: Why do we need a recreation centre?

A. Write <u>who</u>, <u>what</u>, <u>when</u>, <u>where</u>, <u>why</u>, or <u>how</u> to complete each question.

1. _____ will vote on the budget for the recreation centre?

2. _____ will be the various uses of the centre?

3. _____ will the centre be paid for?

4. _____ will the centre be located?

5. _____ do you think a recreation centre is necessary?

6. _____ will the centre be completed?

B. Rewrite the questions below so that they cannot be answered <u>yes</u> or <u>no</u>.

1. Does the park have an interesting history?

_____

2. Is the location of the park good?

_____

3. Does the council have plans to raise local taxes?

_____

4. Will the townspeople have a say on the new recreation centre?

_____

C. Choose a topic and write three questions about it. Remember to begin each question with <u>who</u>, <u>what</u>, <u>when</u>, <u>where</u>, <u>how</u>, or <u>why</u>.

Topic: _____

1. _____

2. _____

3. _____

Unit 5, Composition

> ▪ Many factual articles are based on information gathered in an interview.
> The writer asks questions about the subject he or she wants to cover
> and then uses the information to write an article.

▪ **Read the notes from the interview. Then read the paragraph that Ray and Theresa wrote, and answer the questions that follow.**

Question 1: James, how do you feel about the proposed recreation centre?

Answer: It is definitely needed. The park is too small for our growing city and needs massive repairs anyway. It will be good for the whole city to have a well-equipped recreation centre.

Question 2: Your family has been involved in sports for many years. How do you feel about the modern approach to physical fitness for people of all ages?

Answer: Physical fitness is vital for everyone. That's why the new recreation centre is so important. It will offer facilities and programs for everyone, regardless of age or current fitness levels.

Question 3: What will the recreation centre include?

Answer: The centre will house an indoor pool, a small ice rink, two gyms, meeting rooms, arts-and-crafts facilities, and locker rooms with showers. We also hope to include a weight-lifting room.

> According to Mr. James Leland, park superintendent, the new recreation centre will be a welcome addition to the city's facilities. The old park is now outdated and can no longer fill the needs of the people. Mr. Leland recommends that the park be the site of the new recreation centre. Its facilities, which will include an indoor pool and two gyms, will provide enough variety to fit everyone's needs.

1. Does the author quote Mr. Leland exactly?_____

2. Write one sentence in the article that came from question 1.

   _____

   _____

3. Write one sentence in the article that came from question 3.

   _____

   _____

4. Write another question that Ray could have asked Mr. Leland.

   _____

5. What other things will the recreation centre include that were not in the article?

   _____

Revising and Proofreading

- **Revising** gives you a chance to rethink and review what you have written and to improve your writing. Revise by adding words and information, by taking out unneeded words and information, and by moving words, sentences, and paragraphs around.
- **Proofreading** has to do with checking spelling, punctuation, grammar, and capitalization. Use proofreader's marks to show changes needed in your writing.

Proofreader's Marks

Mark	Meaning
≡	Capitalize.
⊙	Add a period.
✺	Take something out.
/	Make a small letter.
⸌⸍	Add quotation marks.
⟨sp⟩	Correct spelling.
⸜⸝	Add a comma.
∧	Add something.
¶	Indent for new paragraph.
→	Move something.

A. Rewrite the paragraph below. Correct the errors by following the proofreader's marks.

¶ The berryton city council today appruved plans today for construction of a New recreation centre mayor june booth said the centre to be located on the sight of the currant adams park will provide berryton residents with a variety of recreational programs" the centre's facilities include will an indoor pool to gymnasiums arts-and-crafts facilities and a small ice rink and an indoor pool Several meating rooms will also be included too for use buy various organizations.

_____

_____

_____

_____

_____

_____

_____

_____

B. Read the paragraphs below. Use proofreader's marks to revise and proofread the paragraphs. Then write your revised paragraphs below.

Representatives from severals community organizations attended the meeting to express their support of the recreation centre "Construction of this centre is Long Overdue Are members will now have a central place in which to meat instead of crowding into each other's homes said Milton Sayre chair of the berryton citizens senior league

plans call for a groundbreaking ceremony on thursday may 16 at 2 30 followed by a reception in adams park Construction is scheduled mayor booth supervisor john leland and city council members will participate all residents are invited to join them at the ceremoney

_____

_____

_____

_____

_____

_____

_____

_____

_____

_____

_____

_____

_____

_____

A. Expand the sentence bases below by adding adjectives, adverbs, and prepositional phrases.

1. (Friends visited.)

_____

2. (Actors prepared.)

_____

3. (Window broke.)

_____

B. Read the paragraph below. Then circle the topic sentence, and underline only the supporting details.

      Phonograph records have changed over the years. Thomas Edison made them from glass, and he used sound waves to carve the grooves into the records. Edison also invented electricity. Later, phonographic records were made of plastic. Today's compact discs are made of aluminum.

C. Complete the cluster for the topic given in the centre.

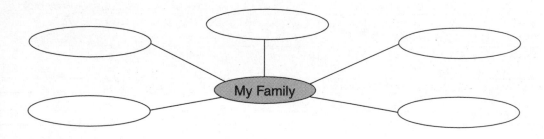

My Family

D. Begin an outline based on that cluster.

Topic: My Family

I. _____

   A. _____

   B. _____

II. _____

   A. _____

   B. _____

E. Number the following sentences in chronological order. Circle any words that indicate chronological order.

_____ Finally, put your ear close to the victim's mouth to be sure that air is coming out of the lungs.

_____ Next, pinch the victim's nostrils together.

_____ Begin by tilting the person's head so that his or her chin points upward.

_____ Then take a deep breath and breathe into the mouth of the victim.

F. Rewrite the interview questions below so that they cannot be answered <u>yes</u> or <u>no</u>.

1. Do you think we need a high-speed train for mass transit in the city?

_____

2. Do you agree that the train should run through town?

_____

3. Will the citizens have any input into the final route?

_____

4. Does the city council have plans to finance the train?

_____

G. Read the paragraph that was written from the interview above. Then answer the questions that follow.

According to Council member Adelia Rodriguez, the city of Centreville needs to build a new high-speed train to serve its citizens in the future. This train would follow a north-south route through the most populated areas of town. The final route would be determined by a panel of experts hired by the city planning commission.

1. Write a sentence that came from interview question 3. _____

_____

2. Which question was not answered in the article? _____

H. Rewrite the paragraph below. Correct the errors by following the proofreader's marks.

¶ once the fog cleared James drove the to the airport to pick up his Sister. When he got their, he discorved the plane was late he asked the ticket person, When will the flight from mexico city arrive the person told him it would be another two hours.

_____

_____

_____

_____

A. Choose a topic in which you are interested.

_____

B. Decide who your audience will be.

_____

C. Write a topic sentence.

_____

D. Draw a cluster diagram for your topic. Draw more circles for supporting details if necessary.

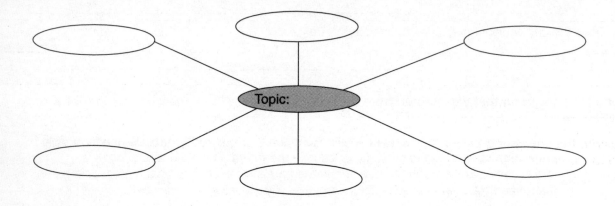

Topic:

E. Write a short outline for a report on your topic.

I. _____

    A. _____

    B. _____

II. _____

    A. _____

    B. _____

III. _____

    A. _____

    B. _____

F. Write five questions about your topic that you would ask if you had an interview with someone who is an expert on the subject.

1. _____

2. _____

3. _____

4. _____

5. _____

G. Write a paragraph with a topic sentence and at least five sentences containing supporting details. Then revise and proofread your paragraph.

_____

_____

_____

_____

_____

_____

_____

H. Rewrite the paragraph below. Correct the errors by following the proofreader's marks. Use the proofreader's marks on page 100 if necessary.

¶ One of the most importantest peaces of fire savety equipment is the smoke detector.

The smoke detector continually all the time monitors the air in you're house. it

sounds an alarm at the first sign of trouble. Fire officials consider the smoke

detectors won of the most best effective low-cost devices alarms available Today.

_____

_____

_____

_____

_____

_____

_____

- A **dictionary** is a reference book that contains definitions of words and other information about their history and use.
- **Entries** in a dictionary are listed in **alphabetical order**.
- **Guide words** appear at the top of each dictionary page. Guide words show the first and last entry on the page.

    EXAMPLE: The word <u>lease</u> would appear on a dictionary page with the guide words <u>learn</u> / <u>lesson</u>. The word <u>lever</u> would not.

A. Put a check in front of each word that would be listed on a dictionary page with the given guide words.

1. fade / flat

_____ faster

_____ face

_____ flavour

_____ fetch

_____ flatter

_____ factory

_____ flag

_____ fancy

_____ flop

_____ fertile

_____ flow

_____ flame

2. image / inform

_____ information

_____ impossible

_____ insect

_____ incomplete

_____ ignore

_____ immense

_____ indeed

_____ improve

_____ insist

_____ infect

_____ imagine

_____ inherit

3. radio / reach

_____ rail

_____ rabbit

_____ ranch

_____ real

_____ raw

_____ raccoon

_____ raft

_____ read

_____ ramp

_____ rate

_____ reduce

_____ rake

B. Number the words in each column in the order of their appearance in a dictionary. Then write the words that could be the guide words for each column.

1. _____ / _____

_____ bedroom

_____ blend

_____ blame

_____ biography

_____ block

_____ blink

_____ bear

_____ benefit

_____ believe

_____ beach

2. _____ / _____

_____ dine

_____ depend

_____ determine

_____ department

_____ district

_____ disease

_____ disturb

_____ discard

_____ difference

_____ dessert

3. _____ / _____

_____ fire

_____ face

_____ free

_____ finger

_____ faint

_____ flower

_____ family

_____ follow

_____ fair

_____ flavour

Dictionary: Syllables

- A **syllable** is a part of a word that is pronounced at one time. Dictionary entry words are divided into syllables to show how they can be divided at the end of a writing line.
- A **midline dot** (·) is placed between syllables to separate them.
  EXAMPLE: quar·ter·back
- If a word has a beginning or ending syllable of only one letter, do not divide it so that one letter stands alone.
  EXAMPLES: a·fraid   bus·y

A. Find each word in a dictionary. Then write each word with a midline dot between each syllable.

1. allowance _____
2. porridge _____
3. harness _____
4. peddle _____
5. character _____
6. hickory _____
7. solution _____
8. variety _____
9. talent _____
10. weather _____

11. brilliant _____
12. enthusiasm _____
13. dramatic _____
14. employment _____
15. laboratory _____
16. judgment _____
17. kingdom _____
18. recognize _____
19. usual _____
20. yesterday _____

B. Write two ways in which each word may be divided at the end of a writing line.

1. victorious   vic·torious   victori·ous
2. inferior   _____   _____
3. quantity   _____   _____
4. satisfactory   _____   _____
5. security   _____   _____
6. possession   _____   _____
7. thermometer   _____   _____
8. getaway   _____   _____

Dictionary: Pronunciation

- Each dictionary entry word is followed by a respelling that shows how the word is **pronounced**.
- An **accent mark** follows a syllable that is said with extra stress. In some words more than one syllable is stressed. The syllable that receives primary stress is followed by a **primary accent mark (´)**. The syllable that receives secondary stress is followed by a **secondary accent mark (´)**.

  EXAMPLE: sub·struc·ture (sub´ struk´ chər)

- A **pronunciation key** (shown below) explains the other symbols used in the respellings.

A. Use the pronunciation key to answer the questions.

1. How many words are given for the symbol ə? _____

2. What symbol is used for the sound of the s in measure? _____

3. What symbol would be used for the sound of a in bar? _____

4. What symbol would be used for the sound of th in whether? _____

5. What symbol would be used for the sound of a in around? _____

6. What symbol would be used for the sound of oo in hoot? _____

hat, āge, fär; let, ēqual, tėrm; it, īce; hot, ōpen, ôrder; oil, out; cup, pût, rüle; əbove, takən, pencəl, lemən, circəs; ch, child; ng, long; sh, ship; th, thin; ᴛʜ, then; zh, measure

B. Use the pronunciation key to help you choose the correct word for each respelling. Underline the correct word.

1. (hēl)   hail   heel   hole
2. (ī´vē)   ivy   I've   eve
3. (ᴛʜ ā)   thee   they   the
4. (let´ ər)   letter   lighter   litter
5. (kāp)   cap   cop   cape
6. (ri tīr´)   retort   retire   writer
7. (ri trēt´)   retreat   retread   retrial
8. (sap)   soap   sip   sap
9. (doun)   den   down   dawn
10. (nü)   no   now   new
11. (hīt)   hit   height   hate
12. (noiz)   nosy   nose   noise
13. (wāt)   what   wit   weight
14. (dī´ə mənd) diamond   demand   depend
15. (ī´ərn)   horn   earn   iron
16. (lēd)   loud   lead   load

                                Unit 6, Study Skills

- A dictionary lists the **definitions** of each entry word. Many words have more than one definition. In this case, the most commonly used definition is given first. Sometimes a definition is followed by a sentence showing a use of the entry word.
- A dictionary also gives the **part of speech** for each entry word. An abbreviation (shown below) stands for each part of speech. Some words may be used as more than one part of speech.

    EXAMPLE: **mess** (mes) *n.* an untidy, usually dirty, condition.
    -v. to make untidy and dirty.

- **Use the dictionary samples below to answer the questions.**

cage (kāj) *n.* a frame or box closed in with wires, bars, etc. *-v.* to lock up or keep in a cage.

cos·tume (kos' tyüm) *n.* **1** a style of dress of a particular time, place, or social class, including garments, hairstyles, etc. **2** a type of dress associated with a particular people, place, or time. *-v.* to provide with a costume.

cot·ton (kot' ən) *n.* **1** soft, downy white or yellowish fibres obtained from the seed pods of any of several closely related plants and used in making fabrics, threads, etc. **2** any of the plants that produce these fibres. **3** thread or cloth made from cotton fibres. *-adj.* made of cotton: *The cotton dress might shrink in warm water.*

1. Which words can be used as either a noun

    or a verb? _____

2. Which word can be used as an adjective?

    _____

3. Which word has the most meanings?

    _____

n.	noun
pron.	pronoun
v.	verb
adj.	adjective
adv.	adverb
prep.	preposition

4. Which word can be used as a noun or as an adjective? _____

5. Write the most commonly used definition of costume. _____

    _____

6. Write a sentence in which you use cage as a verb. _____

    _____

7. Write a sentence using the first definition of costume. _____

    _____

8. Use the second definition of cotton in a sentence. _____

- An **etymology** tells of an entry word's origin and development. Many dictionary entries include an etymology.
- The etymology is usually enclosed in brackets ⟨ ⟩ after the definition of the entry word. The language from which the entry word came into English is listed first, followed by the language from which that word came, and so on. Often the symbol ≤ is used to save space and stands for the phrase "is derived from" or "comes from."

  EXAMPLE: **tu·lip** (tyü´ lip *or* tü´ lip) ⟨ < obs. Du. *tulipa* < Turkish *tülbend* < Persian *dulband* turban ⟩ The word *tulip* came into English from the Dutch word *tulipa*, which came from the Turkish word *tülbend*. The word *tülbend* came from the Persian word *dulband* which meant "turban."

- **Use the dictionary samples below to answer the questions.**

e·mo·tion (i mō´ shən) *n.* strong feeling. ⟨ < F *émotion* (after *motion*) < *émouvoir* stir up < L *emovere* < *e-* out + *movere* move ⟩

gup·py (gup´ ē) *n.* a small, brightly-coloured freshwater fish. ⟨ after Robert J.L. *Guppy,* 19c., of Trinidad, who supplied the first specimens ⟩

line (līn) *n.* a long, narrow mark as with pen or pencil. ⟨ OE *līne* line, rope and F *ligne* line ⟩

load (lōd) *n.* **1** whatever is being carried; a pack, cargo, burden, etc. **2** the amount usually carried at one time; a more or less fixed quantity for a particular type of carrier. ⟨ Old English *lād* carrying ⟩

mar·a·thon (mar´ ə thon´) *n.* a long-distance foot race. ⟨ < *Marathon,* where the Greeks defeated the Persians in 490 B.C. A Greek messenger ran 37 km from Marathon to Athens to bring news of the victory. ⟩

1. Which word comes from the name of a person? _____

2. Which word originally meant "move"? _____

3. Which languages are in the history of the word line? _____

4. Which word comes from Old English? _____

5. Which word comes from the name of a place? _____

6. Which words have more than one language in their histories? _____

7. What is the meaning of the Latin word *emovere*? _____

8. Why is the guppy named after R. J. L. Guppy? _____

9. Why do we call a long race a marathon? _____

_____

10. Which word comes from a word that meant "carrying"? _____

11. Which word comes from the word *ligne*? _____

12. Which words come from French? _____

> - A **title page** lists the name of a book and its author.
> - A **copyright page** tells who published the book, where it was published, and when it was published.
> - A **table of contents** lists the chapter or unit titles and the page numbers on which they begin. It is at the front of a book.
> - An **index** gives a detailed list of the topics in a book and the page numbers on which each topic is found. It is in the back of a book.

A. Answer the questions below.

1. Where should you look for the page number for a particular topic? _____

2. Where should you look to find out who wrote a book? _____

3. Where should you look to get a general idea of the contents of a book? _____

4. Where should you look to find out when a book was published? _____

5. Where should you look to find the name of the book? _____

6. Where should you look to find out who published a book? _____

B. Use your *Language Power* book to answer the questions.

1. What company published this book? _____

2. How many units are in this book? _____

3. On what page does Unit 2 start? _____

4. Where is the index located? _____

5. What is the copyright date? _____

6. What pages contain lessons on pronouns? _____

7. On what page does Unit 5 start? _____

8. On what pages are the lessons on commas found? _____

9. What lesson is on page 86? _____

10. List the pages that teach prepositions. _____

11. On what page is the lesson on guide words found? _____

12. On what page is the lesson on prefixes found? _____

13. On what page does Unit 3 start? _____

Using Visual Aids

- A **chart** lists information in columns, which you read down, and rows, which you read across. The information can be either words or numbers.
- A **graph** shows how quantities change over time. It often shows how two or more things change in relation to one another. The information can be shown through the use of lines, dots, bars, pictures, or in a circle.

A. Use the chart and the graph to answer the following questions.

Library Use Chart

Day of the Week	Science Students	History Students
Monday	18	5
Tuesday	22	16
Wednesday	14	10
Thursday	4	20
Friday	13	15

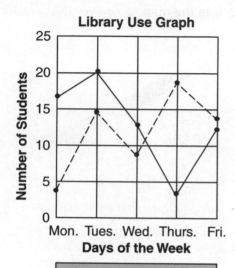

Library Use Graph

Graph Key

Science students ———
History students – – –

1. How many science students used the library on Monday? _____ on Tuesday? _____

   on Wednesday? _____ on Thursday? _____ on Friday? _____

2. Can the question in number 1 be answered by studying the Library Use Chart? _____

   the Library Use Graph? _____

3. On which day was the number of science and history students using the library

   nearly the same? _____

4. On which day did the most science and history students use the library? _____

5. How many science and history students used the library on the day

   mentioned in number 4? _____

6. On which day did the least number of science and history students use the library? _____

Unit 6, Study Skills

- A **road map** is another valuable type of visual aid. Maps like the one shown below are helpful when you are unfamiliar with a certain area. To use any map, you should refer to its **legend**, **compass rose**, and **scale**.
- The legend tells what each symbol represents.
- The compass rose is made up of arrows that point north, south, east, and west.
- The scale allows you to determine how far it is from one location to another. To use the scale, mark the distance between any two locations along the edge of a sheet of paper. Then place the sheet of paper alongside the scale of distance, lining up one of the marks with zero. This will allow you to read the distance between the two locations.

B. **Use the map to answer the questions below.**

Carsonville

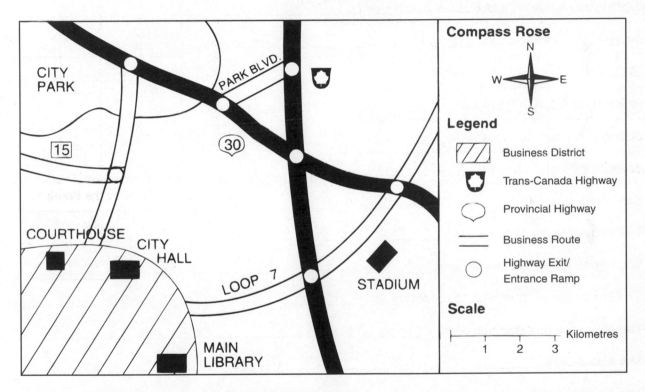

1. Which direction from the business district is City Park? _____

2. On what road is the stadium? _____

3. How many kilometres is it from City Hall to the Main Library? _____

4. What kind of highway is 30? _____

5. Does Business Route 15 run north/south or east/west? _____

6. Is the Courthouse within the business district? _____

7. How many exit ramps are there on Highway 30 from Loop 7 to City Park? _____

8. How many kilometres will you travel if you drive from City Park to the stadium? _____

Using the Library

- Books are arranged on library shelves according to **call numbers**. Each book is assigned a number from 000 to 999, according to its subject matter. The following are the main subject groups for call numbers.

000-099	Reference	500-599	Science and Mathematics
100-199	Philosophy	600-699	Technology
200-299	Religion	700-799	The Arts
300-399	Social Sciences	800-899	Literature
400-499	Languages	900-999	History and Geography

A. Write the call number group in which you would find each book.

1. *1996 World Almanac and Book of Facts* _____

2. *Mathematics for Today* _____

3. *Global Warming: A World Problem* _____

4. *Philosophy Through the Ages* _____

5. *Spanish: A Romance Language* _____

6. *Technology Takes Over* _____

7. *Splitting the Atom* _____

8. *The Encyclopedia of Mammals* _____

9. *The Impressionist School of Painting* _____

10. *Children's Stories from Around the World* _____

11. *The Study of Forgotten Societies* _____

12. *The New Russia* _____

13. *The Religions of the World* _____

14. *The Reader's Guide* _____

15. *Dance in Canada* _____

B. Write the titles of three of your favourite non-fiction books. Write the call number range beside each title.

1. _____

2. _____

3. _____

- The catalogue contains information on every book in the library. Most libraries are now computerized and have on-line catalogues. The information in the computer is filed in the same manner as the information in the older card catalogue.
- Each book has three entries in the catalogue. The entries are filed separately according to: 1. the author's last name, 2. the subject of the book, and 3. the title of the book.
- Most smaller libraries use the **Dewey Decimal System** to organize their books. Each book is assigned a **call number** from 000 to 999, according to its subject matter.

A. Refer to the sample catalogue card to answer the questions about one book.

Subject Card

Call number — 620   **Engineering** — Subject

Author — **Dick, Kris J.**

Title — Technology: the routes of

engineering

Toronto — Place published

Publisher — Gage Educational Publishing Company   1996 — Date published

Number of pages — 60 p.   illus. — Illustrated

1. What is the title? _____

2. Who is the author? _____

3. Who published it? _____ When was it published? _____

4. What is the call number? _____ How many pages does it have? _____

5. What is the general subject? _____

6. Does it contain illustrations? _____

B. Write <u>author</u>, <u>title</u>, or <u>subject</u> to tell which card you would look for to locate the book or books.

1. books about mountain climbing   _____

2. *Life in the Chinese Countryside*   _____

3. a book of short stories by Alice Munro   _____

4. a book by Jane Austen   _____

- An **encyclopedia** is a reference book that contains articles on many different topics. The articles are arranged alphabetically in volumes. Each volume is marked to show which articles are inside.
- Guide words are used to show the first topic on each page.
- At the end of most articles there is a listing of **cross-references** to related topics for the reader to investigate.

A. Find the entry for <u>Henry Norman Bethune</u> in an encyclopedia. Then answer the following questions.

1. What encyclopedia did you use? _____

2. When did Norman Bethune live? _____

3. Where was he born? _____

4. What was his profession? _____

5. For what is he best known? _____

B. Find the entry for <u>Beaver</u> in an encyclopedia. Then answer the following questions.

1. What encyclopedia did you use? _____

2. Where does the beaver live? _____

3. What does it eat? _____

4. Why did the beaver almost die out in the nineteenth century? _____

5. What do they do when alarmed? _____

C. Find the entry in an encyclopedia for a person in whom you are interested. Then answer the following questions.

1. Who is your subject? _____

2. What encyclopedia did you use? _____

3. When did the person live? _____

4. Where did the person live? _____

5. What is it about the person that makes him or her famous? _____

_____

6. What cross-references are listed? _____

Using an Encyclopedia Index

- Most encyclopedias have an **index** of subject titles, listed in alphabetical order. The index shows the volume and the page number where an article can be found. Some encyclopedias contain articles on many different topics. Other encyclopedias contain different articles relating to a broad general topic.

- **Use the sample encyclopedia index to answer the questions below.**

Index

Acorn Squash,1–6; **11**–1759
   Baked, supreme, **1**–7
   Steamed,**1**–7
Appetizer(s), **1**–841; see also Cocktail; Dip; Pickle and Relish; Spread
   Almonds,**1**–89
   Celery, stuffed, **1**–89
   Cheese Ball, **3**–429
Cabbage, **2**–256; see also Salads, Coleslaw; Sauerkraut
   with bacon and cheese sauce,**1**–68
Flour, **5**–705
   Peanut, **8**–1328
   Rice, **10**–1556
   Wheat, **12**–1935

1. In what volume would you find an article on stuffed celery? _____

2. On what page would you find information on cabbage with bacon and cheese sauce? _____

3. Are all articles on flour found in the same volume? _____

4. What are the cross-references for **Appetizers**? _____

5. Do the words in bold show the name of the volume or the name of the main food or ingredient? _____

_____

6. Which main food or ingredient has articles in two volumes? _____

7. Information on which appetizers can be found in the same volume and on the same page? _____

_____

8. What main ingredient is found in Volume 5? _____

9. If you looked under **Dip**, what might you expect to find as a cross-reference? _____

_____

10. Information on what appetizer would be found in Volume 3? _____

11. Information on what ingredient is found on page 1328 in the encyclopedia? _____

> - A **thesaurus** is a reference book that writers use to find the exact words they need. Like a dictionary, a thesaurus lists its entry words alphabetically. Each entry word has a list of **synonyms** *(syn.)*, or words that can be used in its place. Some thesauri also include **antonyms** *(ant.)* for each entry word.
>
>   EXAMPLE: You have just written the following sentence: I was so hungry that I **ate** my lunch quickly. With the help of a thesaurus you could improve your sentence by replacing <u>ate</u> with a more specific synonym, such as <u>devoured</u>. I was so hungry that I **devoured** my lunch quickly.

A. Refer to the sample thesaurus entry below to answer the questions.

> **difficult** *adj.* ***syn.*** puzzling, complex, awkward ***ant.*** simple, effortless

1. Which is the entry word? _____

2. What are its synonyms? _____

3. Which word would you use to describe something complicated? _____

4. Which word would you use to describe something baffling? _____

5. Which word would you use to describe something that might be embarrassing? _____

6. What are the antonyms of <u>difficult</u>? _____

7. Which antonym would you use to describe a test that is easy? _____

B. Use one of the synonyms of <u>difficult</u> to complete each sentence.

1. As an engineer, Marie designs very _____ pieces of machinery.

2. We found ourselves in a very _____ situation when we arrived too early.

3. Manuel is very good at solving _____ mysteries.

C. Write three sentences, each containing a different synonym of <u>difficult</u>.

1. _____

    _____

2. _____

    _____

3. _____

    _____

D. Study the thesaurus entry for <u>talk</u>. Then use a synonym of <u>talk</u> to complete each sentence.

> **talk** *v. syn.* mention, chat, discuss, whisper,
> argue, describe, grumble, say

1. Out of courtesy to others, you should always _____ in a movie theatre.

2. Please _____ your house so that I can find it easily.

3. If you must _____ , you should try not to lose your temper.

4. My sister often likes to _____ with her buddies.

5. Can we _____ the new proposal sometime?

6. You always know the right thing to _____ .

7. My younger brothers always _____ when they're tired and cranky.

8. Did I _____ that I will be gone tomorrow?

E. Write five sentences, each containing a different synonym of <u>talk</u>.

1. _____

2. _____

3. _____

4. _____

5. _____

F. Circle the synonym that best completes each sentence.

1. The batter (looked, glared) at the umpire after his bad call.

2. The (noise, roar) of the crowd was deafening.

3. My brother (aged, matured) after he graduated from high school.

4. My friends often (accumulate, gather) at the park.

5. The man used a (knife, blade) to cut the freshly baked bread.

6. It is my (judgment, opinion) that we all need a holiday now and then.

7. I felt a (loop, knot) in my stomach as I walked up the aisle.

8. I can almost (imagine, think) what it would be like to fly.

9. I (knocked, pushed) the vase over, and water spilled on the floor.

10. I was reading when the tornado (alarm, bell) sounded.

11. I (floated, drifted) to sleep while reading last night.

12. I will miss our cottage after we (leave, abandon) it for the year.

13. We (disguised, hid) our friend's present in her closet.

Using a Periodicals Index

> A **periodical index** allows you to look up magazine articles by author or by subject. Two of the most useful indexes are the *Canadian Periodical Index* and the *Readers' Guide to Periodical Literature.* Both of these are available in book form or on CD-ROM. Use these indexes when you need
> • Recent articles on a particular subject,
> • Several articles written over a period of time about the same subject,
> • Many articles written by the same author.

■ Use the *Canadian Periodical Index* samples to answer the questions.

Subject Entry

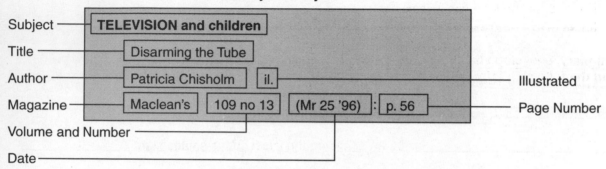

Author Entry

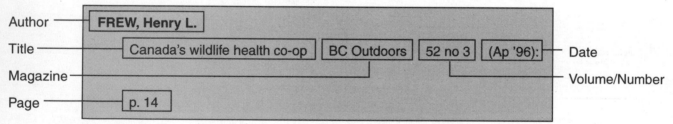

1. Who wrote the article "Canada's Wildlife Health Co-op"? _____

2. In what magazine will you find the article "Disarming the Tube"? _____

3. Who is the author of "Disarming the Tube"? _____

4. In what magazine will you find the article "Canada's Wildlife Health Co-op"? _____

5. Under what subject entry might you find the article "Canada's Wildlife Health Co-op"? _____

6. On what page will you find the article "Disarming the Tube"? _____

7. In what volume of <u>Maclean's</u> does "Disarming the Tube" appear? _____

8. In what month and year was "Disarming the Tube" published? _____

9. What abbreviation is used for the word <u>illustrated</u>? _____

10. In what month and year was "Canada's Wildlife Health Co-op" published? _____

- Use a **dictionary** to find the definitions of words and pronunciations of words, suggestions for word usage, and etymologies.
- Use an **encyclopedia** to find articles about many different people, places, and other subjects. Use an encyclopedia to find references to related subjects.
- Use a **thesaurus** to find synonyms and antonyms.
- Use a **periodical index** to find magazine articles on specific subjects or by particular authors.
- Use an **atlas** to find maps and other information about geographical locations.
- Use an **almanac**, an annual publication, to find such information as population numbers, annual rainfall, election statistics, and other specific information for a given year.

- Write <u>dictionary</u>, <u>encyclopedia</u>, <u>thesaurus</u>, <u>periodical index</u>, <u>atlas</u>, or <u>almanac</u> to show where you would find the following information. Some information may be found in more than one source.

_____ **1.** the life of Queen Elizabeth I

_____ **2.** an article on the latest space shuttle flight

_____ **3.** the provinces and states through which the Rocky Mountains run

_____ **4.** the origin of the word <u>tomato</u>

_____ **5.** the annual rainfall for Somalia

_____ **6.** the most direct route from Spain to Greece

_____ **7.** an antonym for the word <u>happy</u>

_____ **8.** the meaning of the word <u>spar</u>

_____ **9.** recent articles written on the subject of air pollution

_____ **10.** the pronunciation of the word <u>wren</u>

_____ **11.** the life of Sigmund Freud

_____ **12.** a synonym for the word <u>bad</u>

_____ **13.** the years during which World War I was fought

_____ **14.** an article on rock climbing

_____ **15.** the final standings of the National Hockey League for last year

_____ **16.** the meaning of the word <u>history</u>

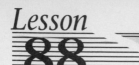

Lesson 88

Using Reference Sources

> ■ Use reference sources—dictionaries, encyclopedias, periodicals indexes, thesauri, atlases, and almanacs—to find information about people, places, or things with which you are not familiar. You can also use these sources to find out more about subjects that interest you.

A. Follow the directions below.

1. Choose a person from history that you would like to know more about.

   Person's name: _____

2. Name two reference sources that you can use to find information about this person.

   a. _____

   b. _____

3. Use one of the reference sources you named above. Find the entry for the person you are researching. Write the exact title of the reference.

   _____

4. Write a short summary of the information you found.

   _____

   _____

   _____

   _____

5. Name the source that would contain recent articles about this person.

6. Look up your person's name in the reference source you listed in number 5. Write the titles of three articles that were listed.

   a. _____

   b. _____

   c. _____

7. Which of the articles above, if any, can be found in your library?

   _____

8. Name a subject heading under which you might find more information on your person.

   _____

                      Unit 6, Study Skills

B. Follow the directions, and answer the questions.

1. Choose a country you would like to know more about.

   Name of country: _____

2. List four reference sources that you can use to find information about this country.

   a. _____   c. _____

   b. _____   d. _____

3. Find the entry for the country in one of the reference sources you listed.

   Write the exact title of the reference source.

4. Write a short summary of the information you found.

   _____

   _____

   _____

   _____

   _____

5. Find the entry for the country in one other reference source. Write the exact title of the reference source.

   _____

6. What new information did you find about the country?

   _____

   _____

   _____

C. Follow the directions, and answer the questions below.

1. In what province do you live? _____

2. Find the entry for your province in one of the reference sources. Write the exact

   title of the reference source. _____

3. Write a short summary of the information you found about your province.

   _____

   _____

   _____

   _____

© 1997 Gage Educational Publishing Company

Review

A. Use the dictionary samples below to answer the questions.

ex·pose (ek spōz´) *v.* **1** to leave open; leave unprotected; uncover; make vulnerable or liable: *His foolish actions exposed him to ridicule.* **2** make known. **3** *Photography.* allow light to reach and act on (a sensitive film, plate, or paper). ⟨ < OF *exposer* < *ex-* forth (< L *ex-*) + *poser* put ⟩

ex·po·si·tion (ek spə zish´ ən) *n.* **1** a public show or exhibition. **2** a detailed explanation: *the exposition of a scientific theory.*

ex·press (ek spres´) *v.* **1** put into words: *Express your ideas clearly.* **2** show by look, voice, or action; reveal: *Your smile expresses joy.* **3** send by express. ⟨ < L *expressus*, pp. of *exprimere* < *ex-* out + *premere* press ⟩

ex·qui·site (ek skwiz´ it) *adj.* **1** very lovely in a delicate way: *exquisite lace. Violets are exquisite flowers.* **2** of highest excellence; most admirable: *an exquisite painting technique.* ⟨ < L *exquisitus*, pp. of *exquirere* < *ex-* out + *quaerere* seek ⟩

1. Underline the words that could be guide words for the dictionary page above.

   a. expel / expire   c. export / extend

   b. expand / expense   d. extra / extreme

2. What part of speech is expose? _____ exposition? _____ express? _____

3. How many syllables does the word exposition have? _____ express? _____

4. Write the correct word for each respelling.

   a. (ek skwiz´ it) _____   c. (ek spə zish´ ən) _____

   b. (ek spōz´) _____   d. (ek spres´) _____

5. What word comes from the Latin word expressus? _____

6. From what two languages does the word expose come?

   _____   _____

7. Write one sentence in which you use express according to its second definition.

   _____

8. What word comes from a Latin word that means "to seek out"? _____

B. Write title page, copyright page, table of contents, or index to tell where to find this information.

_____ 1. the author's name

_____ 2. the chapter titles

_____ 3. the year the book was published

_____ 4. the page number on which a particular topic can be found

_____ 5. the publisher's name

_____ 6. the book's title

C. Use the map to answer the questions.

Franklin Point

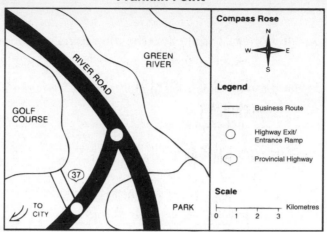

1. Which direction is the city from the park? _____

2. What kind of highway is 37? _____

3. How far is it from the exit on River Road to the golf course? _____

D. Use the sample thesaurus entry below to answer the questions.

> **activity** *n. syn.* action, movement, motion
> ***ant.*** inactivity, inaction, motionlessness

1. What is the entry word? _____

2. What are its antonyms? _____

E. Use the periodicals index sample to answer the questions.

> **CAME, Barry**
> Finding common ground in Québec. il. *Maclean's* 109 no. 14 (Ap 1 '96): p. 22

1. What is the title of the article? _____

2. In what magazine does the article appear? _____

3. On what page will you find the article? _____

F. Write dictionary, encyclopedia, thesaurus, periodical index, atlas, or almanac to show where you would find the following information.

1. the most direct route from Calgary, Alberta, to Albuquerque, New Mexico _____

2. the pronunciation of the word sedentary _____

3. an antonym for the word bright _____

4. the life of Indira Gandhi _____

5. the increase in world population last year _____

© 1997 Gage Educational Publishing Company

Using What You've Learned

A. Find the word <u>humour</u> in your dictionary. Then follow the directions and answer the questions.

1. Write the guide words from the page on which you found the entry for <u>humour</u>. _____

2. Write <u>humour</u> in syllables. _____

3. As what parts of speech can <u>humour</u> be used? _____

4. Write the history of the word. _____

_____

B. Use the sample catalogue entry to answer the questions.

> 650.1
> **Fuller, J. Michael**
>   Above the bottom line: building business success through
> individual growth.
> Toronto, Macmillan Canada, Colonial Press [1993]   350 p.   illus.

1. What type of catalogue entry is this?

   a. subject   **b.** author   **c.** title

2. What is the call number of the book? _____

3. What is the title of the book? _____

4. Is the book illustrated? _____

C. Use the encyclopedia sample to answer the questions.

> **CREE** is the tribal name of a group of First Nations people now living on reservations in Canada. They were originally forest hunters and trappers who traded with the early French and English fur traders. Part of the group moved southwest and became known as Plains Cree. See also NATIVE AMERICANS.

1. What is the article about? _____

2. Where did some members of the tribe move? _____

3. Under what subject heading can you find related information? _____

_____

D. Use the periodicals index sample to answer the questions.

> **DEACON, James**
> Even Great Ones Get the Blues. il. *Maclean's* 109
> no 11 (Mr 11 '96): p46–7

1. What is the title of the article? _____

2. Who is the author? _____

3. In what magazine does the article appear? _____

E. Use a thesaurus to find a synonym for each underlined word.

_____ 1. My milk shake was so <u>large</u> that I couldn't finish it.

_____ 2. The police <u>found</u> our stolen property.

F. Use the information in the chart to complete the graph. Then answer the questions.

Club Membership

Chart

Year	Men	Women
1960	40	40
1970	30	10
1980	20	30
1990	30	30

Graph

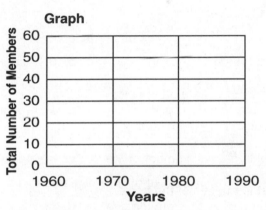

1. How many women belonged to the club in 1960? _____

2. What was the total number of members in 1960? _____

3. What two years had an equal number of members? _____

G. Use the sample encyclopedia index entry to answer the questions.

> **Generation(s), 5-**877; *See also* Families; Grandparents

1. In what volume is the article on generations? _____

2. On what page does the article begin? _____

Synonyms and Antonyms ▪ On the line before each pair of words, write <u>S</u> if they are synonyms, or <u>A</u> if they are antonyms.

_____ **1.** brave, courageous   _____ **4.** late, early   _____ **7.** begin, end

_____ **2.** start, commence   _____ **5.** smile, grin   _____ **8.** country, nation

_____ **3.** happy, unhappy   _____ **6.** quick, slow   _____ **9.** sweet, sour

Homonyms ▪ Underline the correct homonyms in each sentence below.

1. Tina went (by, buy)(plain, plane) to visit her (ant, aunt).

2. We had a (great, grate) talk with the school (principle, principal).

3. The kitten had white (hair, hare), large (pause, paws), and a long (tail, tale).

Homographs ▪ Circle the letter for the best definition for each underlined homograph.

1. Lee ate the <u>rest</u> of the meatball sandwich.

    a. part left over   **b.** inactive period of time

2. The heat in the <u>desert</u> was unbearable.

    a. to abandon   **b.** dry, barren land

3. Dana's <u>club</u> had a car wash to raise money for their trip.

    a. a heavy wooden stick   **b.** an organization of people

4. The room is <u>light</u> because it has many windows.

    a. bright   **b.** not heavy

5. Please <u>tear</u> the article out of the magazine for me.

    a. a drop of water from the eye   **b.** rip

Prefixes, Suffixes, and Compound Words ▪ Write <u>P</u> if the underlined word has a prefix, write <u>S</u> if it has a suffix, and write <u>C</u> if it is a compound word.

1. _____ _____   Tony was <u>careful</u> as he walked <u>uphill</u> to the soggy field.

2. _____ _____   It seemed awfully wet for the <u>softball</u> game. He was not <u>hopeful</u>.

3. _____ _____   He began to <u>rethink</u> his decision to play. Perhaps he had been <u>foolish</u>.

4. _____ _____   His <u>teammates</u> would be <u>helpless</u> in this mud.

5. _____ _____   The other team felt <u>unhappy</u>. They said running could be <u>hazardous</u>.

6. _____ _____   Suddenly there was a <u>downpour</u>. They would be <u>unable</u> to play.

7. _____ _____   They decided to <u>reschedule</u> the game for the next Thursday <u>afternoon</u>.

8. _____ _____   Tony's team was <u>thankful</u> for the delay. They needed the <u>weekend</u> for extra practice.

9. _____ _____   The game is an important one for <u>everyone</u>. Neither team's <u>pitcher</u> has lost a game yet.

Contractions ▪ Write the contraction for each pair of words.

1. I am _____

2. would not _____

3. do not _____

4. I have _____

5. you have _____

6. is not _____

7. will not _____

8. does not _____

9. I will _____

10. they are _____

11. had not _____

12. there is _____

Connotation and Denotation ▪ For each underlined word, write (–) for a negative connotation, (+) for a positive connotation, or (N) for a neutral connotation.

_____ 1. Jake told us a <u>story</u> at the party.

_____ 2. Jake is such a <u>showoff</u>.

_____ 3. He <u>brags</u> about his sense of humour.

_____ 4. Often he tells a <u>hilarious</u> story.

_____ 5. This story was <u>dull</u>.

_____ 6. In fact, I got <u>bored</u>, so I left.

_____ 7. I went home and fell <u>asleep</u>.

_____ 8. I slept <u>peacefully</u> all night.

_____ 9. Sue <u>giggled</u> at the joke.

_____ 10. She <u>wept</u> at the last act.

_____ 11. Suddenly he <u>snarled</u>.

_____ 12. The <u>curtain</u> came down.

_____ 13. We <u>plodded</u> home.

_____ 14. We ate <u>delicious</u> muffins.

Idioms ▪ Underline the idioms in each sentence. Then write the meaning of the idiom on the line.

1. The band's new song didn't knock my socks off.

_____

2. I was out like a light the moment my head hit the pillow.

_____

3. He flew off the handle when he learned his car had been stolen.

_____

4. Her smile lit up the sky.

_____

5. Makoto let the cat out of the bag when he mentioned the surprise party.

_____

6. She was down in the dumps after she missed the speech.

_____

7. The good news from his sister put him on cloud nine.

_____

8. She was on the fence about the invitation.

_____

Types of Sentences ▪ Before each sentence, write D for declarative, IN for interrogative, IM for imperative, and E for exclamatory. Write X if it is not a sentence. Punctuate each sentence correctly.

1. _____ Oh, the road is closed ___

2. _____ What should we do now ___

3. _____ Stop talking and let me think ___

4. _____ We must find a new road ___

5. _____ Need to turn around ___

6. _____ I'll pull over to the side of the road ___

7. _____ Get the map that's on the back seat ___

8. _____ I can find an alternate route ___

Subjects and Predicates ▪ Draw a line between the complete subject and the complete predicate in each sentence below. Write SS for a simple subject, CS for a compound subject, SP for a simple predicate, and CP for a compound predicate.

_____ _____ 1. Steve washed and waxed his car.

_____ _____ 2. Steve's sister and brother helped him polish the chrome.

_____ _____ 3. The sky-blue car shone in the sun.

_____ _____ 4. Steve keeps his car in good condition.

_____ _____ 5. Steve and his neighbour work on the car every weekend.

_____ _____ 6. Both young men are taking an auto mechanics course and practise on Steve's car.

_____ _____ 7. The car looks great and runs beautifully.

_____ _____ 8. Steve and his neighbour both love that car.

Compound Sentences ▪ Combine each pair of sentences below to form a compound sentence.

1. Jason wasn't sure what to do. Samia wasn't helping with her suggestions.

_____

2. He listened to what Susan said. Her ideas just wouldn't work.

_____

3. It was getting dark. They needed to leave soon.

_____

4. Jason had an idea. Samia agreed with the idea.

_____

Direct Objects and Indirect Objects ▪ Underline the verb in each sentence. Then write DO above the direct object and IO above the indirect object.

1. The store gave the contest winner a free trip.

2. The coach bought his soccer team pepperoni pizzas.

3. Tomas handed the taxi driver a generous tip.

Correcting Run-on Sentences and Expanding Sentences ▪ Correct the run-on sentence. Then expand each new sentence by adding details.

George ran down the track, he was in the lead.

_____

_____

Independent and Subordinate Clauses ▪ Underline the independent clause, and circle the subordinate clause in each sentence below. Describe the subordinate clause by writing <u>adjective clause</u> or <u>adverb clause</u> on the line before each sentence.

_____ 1. The paintings we saw at the museum were beautiful.

_____ 2. Before Cathy went to university, she travelled for a year.

_____ 3. Employees who work the night shift at the plant receive extra pay.

_____ 4. Marla found her missing keys when she was searching for her briefcase.

_____ 5. The landlord remodelled our apartment after we signed the new lease.

_____ 6. Félix Leclerc was a famous Québec singer-songwriter who also wrote plays.

_____ 7. The dresser we saw at the garage sale was a valuable antique.

_____ 8. Gaston volunteered at the community centre because he liked helping children.

_____ 9. We stopped delivery of the newspaper and the mail since we were going away for a month.

Complex Sentences ▪ Insert the subordinate clause in parentheses into the independent clause to form a complex sentence. Write the complex sentence on the line.

1. (who specializes in cancer research) The doctor spoke to the medical students.

_____

2. (when he arrives at his destination) Mr. Burris will notify the office.

_____

3. (where we do our research) The library is closed for repairs all week.

_____

4. (which has been closed for safety reasons) The coal mine will begin operating again next month.

_____

Parts of Speech ▪ Write the part of speech above each underlined word. Use the abbreviations given in the box.

1. We had grilled steak, baked potatoes, and a fresh tossed salad for dinner.

2. The exhausted hikers quickly set up their tents and went to sleep.

3. The Japanese gardener pruned the young fruit trees and rose bushes carefully.

4. Isaac tried very hard to finish the mystery novel, but he fell asleep.

5. The island's tourists quietly watched the glorious sunset until it disappeared.

n.	noun
pron.	pronoun
v.	verb
adj.	adjective
adv.	adverb
prep.	preposition

Verbs ▪ Underline the correct verb, and circle the verbal in each sentence.

1. Gardening (is, are) Mr. and Mrs. Butala's favourite hobby.

2. Dean (received, will receive) his swimming medal tomorrow.

3. We (driven, drove) to the lake to fish for trout.

4. The pitcher (has tried, have tried) to throw the runner out.

5. Roberto (chose, chosen) to wait in line for a ticket.

6. The thief (broken, broke) into the office to steal equipment.

7. Jocelyn (have decided, has decided) to move to a new town.

8. The dried spices (smells, smell) wonderful.

Pronouns ▪ Underline the pronoun in parentheses that agrees with the antecedent in each sentence. Circle each antecedent.

1. Scott's brothers gave him (their, his) suggestions.

2. The children took care of the wounded bird and then set (them, it) free.

3. The coach was interviewed by reporters after (his, their) game.

Adjectives and Adverbs ▪ Complete each sentence with the proper form of the adjective or adverb in parentheses.

1. (early) We arrived at the party _____ than the other guests.

2. (expensive) The groceries for the cookout were _____ than the ones

    for the birthday party.

3. (tall) Is Lei the _____ player on the basketball team?

4. (fresh) Use this loaf of bread for the sandwiches since it is _____ than mine.

Manatees _____ mammals whose population is endangered. Also
(linking verb)

known as sea cows, manatees have dark grey skin, a very small head, poorly developed

eyes that _____ see _____ , and two front
(contraction of do) (adverb)

flippers. _____ tails are large, rounded flippers. Manatees live
(possessive pronoun)

_____ shallow, fresh water or salt water and eat underwater plants.
(preposition)

They _____ in the southeastern part _____
(intransitive verb) (preposition)

the United States, western Africa, South America, the Amazon, and the Caribbean Sea.

Manatees are _____ gentle animals. _____
(adverb) (gerund of rub)

muzzles is how they communicate. If alarmed, _____ make a
(subject pronoun)

_____ noise. By adulthood, they grow to between two and five metres
(present participle of chirp)

_____ weigh _____ 130 kilograms. Scientists
(conjunction) (adverb)

studying _____ adult manatee _____ observed
(limiting adjective) (helping verb)

that it can eat about 45 kilograms of plants in one day.

Manatees _____ clean waterways by eating vegetation before it blocks
(helping verb)

narrow passages. In some areas, manatees are encouraged _____
(infinitive of thrive)

so they _____ waterways free of plants. Boats and boat propellers
(future tense of keep)

are the _____ enemy of the manatee. In a few places, people hunt
(superlative adjective)

_____ for meat, oil, and hides. _____
(object pronoun) (demonstrative adjective)

hunting has led to the decline of the manatee population. _____ ,
(conjunction)

in most areas, manatees _____ by law.
(protect in passive voice)

Capitalization and End Punctuation ▪ Circle each letter that should be capitalized. Write the capital letter above it. Add correct end punctuation to each sentence.

1. the road rally will start on nov. 1 in windsor, ontario ___

2. tom asked, "how many italian sports cars will be entered ___"

3. dr. smith plans to enter betsy, his antique ford ___

4. "wow, betsy is the best antique car in the rally!" said mr. lane ___

5. they heard there might be a special entry from japan ___

6. tom asked, "are you sure the entry arrived before the deadline on monday ___"

7. mr. lane said, "no, but i did see an address from kyoto, japan, with the list of competitors ___"

8. "betsy will have no trouble beating the competition," said tom ___

Commas ▪ Add commas where needed in the sentences below.

1. Yes we have visited Japan France and Italy.

2. After we picked up Pepe my poodle from the groomer we took him to the veterinarian.

3. Well I think the judge showed compassion integrity and fairness in the courtroom.

4. Bill the rehearsal is beginning and we need you to join us now.

5. Belinda my oldest sister earns extra money by running errands sewing and cooking for our neighbour.

6. Jeff please finish your report and I will type it for you.

Quotation Marks and Commas ▪ Add quotation marks and commas where needed in the sentences below.

1. Tony said Meg I saw your dog in Kevin's yard.

2. Julio the telegram is for you called his brother.

3. Mr. Simpson asked What time does the softball game begin?

4. Ms. Ito asked the reporter are you going to run for mayor?

5. Our company is on McNeil Road replied the receptionist.

6. You need to improve your defence said Coach Stitsky if you expect to win the big game.

 Capitalization and Punctuation

Apostrophes ▪ Insert apostrophes where they are needed in the sentences below.

1. I cant find the consultants report anywhere.

2. The teams new uniforms werent sewn properly.

3. Doesnt that store sell womens jewellery?

4. The horses owner wouldnt sell them for any price.

5. Cant you pick up Stephanies car for her at the repair shop?

Colons and Hyphens ▪ Add colons and hyphens where they are needed in the sentences below.

1. Our meeting is at 130 this afternoon, and you need to remind the fol

lowing people Jim Brown, Patricia West, Ann Tyler, and Jeff Ray.

2. My brother in law helped us move into our second storey apartment.

3. Between 100 and 500 yesterday, twenty five people signed the sign up sheet for

the conference.

4. That well known Italian restaurant specializes in the following foods lasagna,

grilled shrimp, veal, and spaghetti with meatballs.

5. My great grandfather will be eighty seven years old tomorrow.

Punctuation and Capitalization ▪ Circle each letter that should be capitalized below. Add commas, question marks, quotation marks, apostrophes, periods, colons, and hyphens where needed.

3720 w. anderson
corner brook, nf a2h 5m3
may 7, 1997

ms. jean jackson
735 w. 79th street
windsor, on n9e 1p7

Dear ms. jackson

    i want to enter my antique ford betsy in the International Car Rally to be held august 12, 1997 ___ please send me any information i may need to register ___ i understand you only accept seventy five entries ___ am i too late ___ i was told to wait until may to inquire so i hope there are still openings ___

    a friend who has entered in the past said this is the best rally of the whole year ___ im excited about entering ___ my car is a 1910 classic in excellent condition ___ it has won numerous awards over the years and it is not ready to retire ___ my wife and i are looking forward to the drive from our home in newfoundland all the way to windsor ___ were studying travel brochures on ontario in anticipation of our visit ___ ill be waiting to hear from you ___

Sincerely yours,
dr. lee smith

Composition ▪ Read the paragraphs. Then answer the questions that follow.

In order to prove that shipwrecked sailors could survive in an open boat at sea, Dr. Bombard decided to conduct an experiment. First, he chose a four-and-a-half metre open rubber boat. Then he decided not to take any food or water with him. Since most shipwrecked sailors die from lack of food or water, he wanted to find a way to survive strictly off the sea. Finally, on October 19, 1953, Dr. Bombard started his journey across the Atlantic Ocean.

Dr. Bombard discovered two very important things on his journey. The most important was that sailors could drink seawater. This was something that many felt would speed death instead of helping people to live. Dr. Bombard drank over a pint of seawater every day and lived to tell about it. His next important discovery was that he could keep from getting diseases caused by lack of proper vitamins by eating plankton. Plankton are small, vitamin-rich plants and animals that float in the sea. Many sea creatures live on plankton. Eating just a teaspoon or so of plankton a day gave him all the vitamins and minerals he needed. He also ate raw fish that he caught daily. Although he lost 25 kilograms, Dr. Bombard proved that sailors could survive by living off the sea.

1. Underline the topic sentence in each paragraph.

2. How many supporting details are in the first paragraph? _____ in the second? _____

3. Is the first paragraph written in chronological order or spatial order? _____

4. Write the time order words found in the first paragraph.

   _____   _____   _____

5. What is the topic of the selection? _____

6. Write one possible audience that might be interested in the selection.

   _____

7. Complete the outline for the selection.

   I. Dr. Bombard gets ready

      A. _____

      B. _____

   II. Discoveries

      A. _____

      B. _____

8. Write two questions you would ask Dr. Bombard in an interview.

   a._____

   b._____

Clustering ▪ Read the paragraph. Underline the topic sentence. Then fill in the cluster to show how the details relating to that topic sentence could have been chosen.

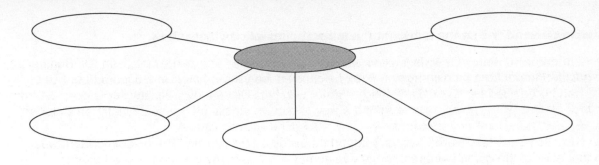

The birth of the island of Surtsey was a violent event. First, a large, black cloud burst from the water. A rumbling sound came from under the ocean. The cloud grew to 3600 metres high. Giant explosions spewed ash, dust, and hot rocks. A mountain rose from the water. A volcano in the ocean had erupted.

Revising and Proofreading ▪ Read the paragraphs below. Use proofreader's marks to revise and proofread the paragraphs. Then write your revised paragraphs.

An avalanche is a fast-mooving pile of Snow that falls down a mountain a sound such as like a yell or a gun fireing, can be enough to set won off. Each year, seven people about will be killed in an avlanche in canada sometimes, people are traped in are pokets under under the snow, and can suvive for howrs or even days Rescyuers use long Poles to try to find them.

_____

_____

_____

_____

_____

_____

_____

_____

_____

_____

Using the Dictionary ▪ Use the dictionary samples to answer the questions.

earn (ėrn) *v.* **1** receive in return for work or service done. *She earns ten dollars an hour.* **2** do enough work for; deserve; be worth: *He is paid more than he really earns.* ⟨ OE *earnian* ⟩

earth (ėrth) *n.* **1** the third planet from the sun, and the fifth in size. **2** dry land. **3** ground; soil; dirt: *The earth in the garden is soft* ⟨ OE *eorthe* ⟩

1. Circle the letter of the guide words for the above entry.

   a. east / ebb   **b.** each / easily   **c.** each / eagle

2. How many definitions are listed for earn? _____ earth? _____

3. Write one sentence using the second definition of earth.

   _____

4. Write the most commonly used definition of earn. _____

   _____

5. What part of speech is earn? _____ earth? _____

6. How many syllables do earn and earth have? _____

7. Write the respelling of earn. _____ earth. _____

8. Which word came from the Old English word earnian? _____

Parts of a Book ▪ Write title page, copyright page, table of contents, or index to tell where you would find this information.

_____ **1.** The page on which specific information can be found

_____ **2.** The author's name

_____ **3.** The page on which a chapter begins

_____ **4.** The year the book was published

Reference Sources ▪ Write D for dictionary, E for encyclopedia, TH for thesaurus, AL for almanac, AT for atlas, or PI for periodicals index to tell where you would find this information.

_____ **1.** an article on the Toronto Blue Jays   _____ **4.** the distance between Rome and Naples

_____ **2.** the etymology of the word baseball   _____ **5.** a synonym for the word build

_____ **3.** the history of the Red Cross   _____ **6.** planning a vegetable garden

Using Visual Aids ▪ Use the map to answer the questions.

1. What direction is the museum from the police station?

    _____

2. How far is it from the museum to the recreation centre?

    _____

3. Does First Street run north/south or east/west?

    _____

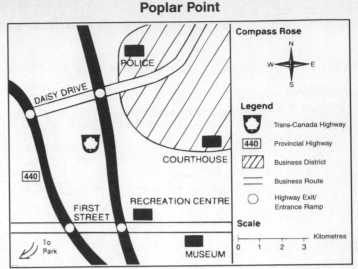

Poplar Point

Compass Rose

Legend

⬭ Trans-Canada Highway
[440] Provincial Highway
▨ Business District
— Business Route
○ Highway Exit/ Entrance Ramp

Scale
0 1 2 3 Kilometres

Using the Library Catalogue ▪ Use the sample catalogue entry to answer the questions.

Author Entry

> 909.07
> **Haberman, Arthur**
>   Civilizations – Toronto: Gage, 1994   96 p.

1. Who is the author? _____

2. What is the book's call number? _____

3. Who is the book's publisher? _____

Using a Thesaurus • Use the sample thesaurus entry to answer the questions.

> **produce** *v. syn.* bear, yield, give, cause, make *ant.* waste, destroy

1. What is the entry word? _____

2. What part of speech is <u>produce</u>? _____

3. What are its synonyms? _____

Using a periodicals index ▪ Use the periodicals index sample to answer the questions.

> **SWINE industry**
>   Clean, green and not so smelly. Michelle Knott. il.
> New Scientist 149 no 2022 (Mr 16 '96): p 20

1. Who is the author of this article? _____

2. On what page is the article? _____

3. Is the article illustrated? _____

Index

Abbreviations, 79, 88
Accent marks, 108
Adjectives
  demonstrative, 66, 76, 133
  limiting, 65, 133
  proper, 65, 76, 78, 80
  recognizing, 65, 74, 76, 132
  that compare, 67, 76, 132, 133
  using, 65, 91, 102, 133
Adverbs
  recognizing, 68, 74, 132
  that compare, 69, 132
  using, 68, 91, 102, 133
Almanac, 121, 122–123, 125, 138
Antecedents, 64, 75, 132
Antonyms, 1, 10, 12, 128
Apostrophes, 85, 88, 89–90, 135
Appositives, 44, 74
Atlas, 121, 122–123, 125, 138

Book, parts of, 111, 124, 138

Capitalization, 78–80, 85, 87–88, 89–90, 134, 135
Card catalogue, 115, 126, 139
Clauses
  adjective, 27, 34, 131
  adverb, 28, 34, 131
  independent, 26, 29, 30, 34, 35–36, 131
  subordinate, 26–28, 30, 34, 35–36, 83, 131
Clustering, 96, 102, 104, 137
Colons, 86, 88, 135
Commas
  in complex sentences, 83–84, 87, 89–90, 134
  in compound sentences, 29, 83–84, 87–90, 134
  in quotations, 83–85, 87, 134
  in series, 83–84, 87–88, 89–90, 134
  to set off appositives, 84, 87, 134
  to set off name of person being addressed, 84, 87, 134
  using, 83–84,87–90, 134, 135
Compound words, 7, 11, 86, 128
Conjunctions, 28, 73, 74, 76, 132–133
Connotation/Denotation, 8, 11, 13, 129
Contractions, 6, 11, 12, 57, 85, 129

Dewey Decimal System, 115
Dictionary, 106–110, 121–126, 138

Direct objects, 24, 25, 33–35, 58, 130

Encyclopedia, 116, 117, 121–123, 125–127, 138
Etymology, 110, 124, 138
Exclamation points,15–16, 82, 87, 89–90, 134

Gerunds, 59–60, 75, 133

Homographs, 3, 10, 12, 128
Homonyms, 2, 10, 12, 128
Hyphens, 86, 88, 135

Idioms, 9, 11, 13, 129
Indirect objects, 25, 33, 34, 35, 130
Infinitives, 59–60, 75, 133
Interjections, 82
Interviews, 98, 99, 103, 105, 136

Library, using, 114, 139

Nouns
  common, 38–39
  plural, 40–41, 74, 77
  possessive, 42–43, 74, 77, 85
  proper, 38–39, 78–80
  recognizing, 37, 44, 74, 132–133
  singular, 40–41

Outlining, 97, 102, 104, 136

Paragraphs
  audience of, 95, 104, 136
  ordering information within, 94, 103, 136
  supporting details in, 93, 96, 102, 104–105, 136–137
  topic of, 95, 96, 104, 136–137
  topic sentences in, 92, 93, 96, 102, 104–105, 136–137
Participles, 59–60, 75, 133
Periodicals Index, 120–123, 125, 127, 138–139
Periods,15–16, 81–82, 87–90, 134, 135
Predicates
  complete, 17–18, 22, 33, 35, 130
  compound, 22, 23, 33, 35, 130
  simple, 19, 22, 33, 130
Prefixes, 4, 10, 12, 128
Prepositional phrases, 71, 72, 76, 91, 102
Prepositions, 70, 74, 132–133
Pronouns
  antecedents for, 64, 75, 132
  indefinite, 62–64

  object, 62–63, 133
  possessive, 62–63, 133
  recognizing, 62–64, 74, 76, 132, 133
  relative, 27
  subject, 62–63, 133
  using, 75, 77, 133
Pronunciation key, 108
Question marks, 15–16, 81–82, 87, 89–90, 134, 135
Quotation marks, 85, 87, 134, 135
Revising/Proofreading, 100–101, 103, 105, 137
Sentences
  combining, 23, 34, 35
  complex, 30, 33, 36, 131
  compound, 29, 31, 33–35, 130
  expanding, 32, 34, 36, 91, 102, 131
  inverted, 20, 34, 36
  recognizing, 14, 130
  run–on, 31, 34, 36, 131
  simple, 29 types of, 15–16, 33, 35, 130
Subjects
  complete, 17–18, 22, 33, 35, 130
  compound, 21, 23, 33, 35, 130
  position of, 20
  simple, 19, 21, 33, 35, 130
Suffixes, 5, 10, 12, 128
Synonyms, 1, 10, 12, 128
Thesaurus, 118–119, 121–123, 125, 127, 138–139
Usage, 51–57, 75
Verbals, 59–60, 75, 132, 133
Verbs
  action, 45
  helping, 48, 54–57, 133
  intransitive, 58, 133
  linking, 46, 133
  perfect tenses, 50
  phrases, 48
  principal parts of, 47
  recognizing, 24, 25, 34, 45–46, 74, 130, 132, 133
  tenses, 49–57, 75, 132–133
  transitive, 58, 133
  using, 51, 133
  voice, 61, 133
Visual aids, 112, 113, 125, 127, 139
Writing process. *See* Paragraphs.

140